THE WAFFEN-SS IN POLAND, 1939

CASEMATE | ILLUSTRATED

CASEMATE | ILLUSTRATED

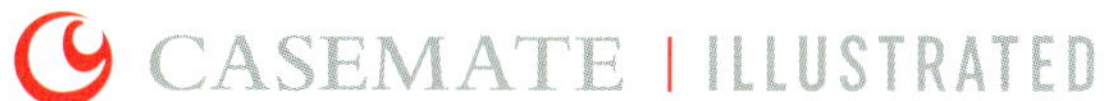

THE WAFFEN-SS IN POLAND, 1939

MASSIMILIANO AFIERO

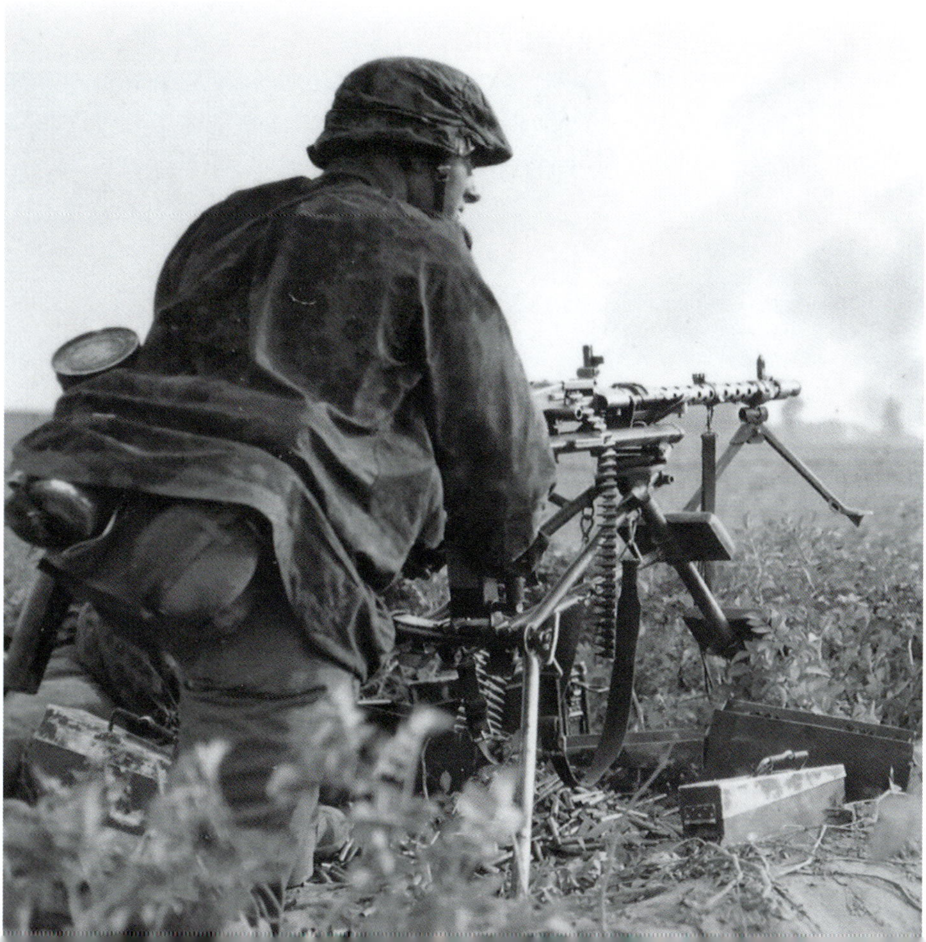

CASEMATE | ILLUSTRATED

CIS0048

Published in 2025 by
CASEMATE PUBLISHERS
1950 Lawrence Road, Havertown, PA 19083, USA
and
47 Church Street, Barnsley, S70 2AS, UK

Print Edition: ISBN 978-1-63624-465-5
Digital Edition: ISBN 978-1-63624-466-2

Originally published in Italian as *Fall Weiss: I reparti combattenti SS in Polonia settembre 1939* by Massimiliano Afiero © Associazione Cultural Ritterkreuz, 2019

Translated by Ralph Riccio
Additional text by Chris Cocks
Design by Battlefield Design
Maps created by Battlefield Design
Artwork by Battlefield Design

Printed and bound in the Czech Republic by FINIDR s.r.o.

CASEMATE PUBLISHERS (US)
Telephone (610) 853-9131
Fax (610) 853-9146
Email: casemate@casematepublishers.com
www.casematepublishers.com

CASEMATE PUBLISHERS (UK)
Telephone (0)1226 734350
Email: casemate@casemateuk.com
www.casemateuk.com

Photographic credits: Bundesarchiv, Germania (BA); Washington, D.C. National Archives and Records Administration (NA); Berlin Document Center (BDC); Istituto di Storia Moderna di Lubiana (MZNS); Deutsche Wochenschau (DW) films; Imperial War Museums (IWM); Munin Verlag; Massimiliano Afiero (MA); Carlo Fattoretto (CF); Giorgio Bussano (GB); Pierre Tiquet (PT); Charles Trang (CT).

Title page image: An SS-Deutschland MG 34 on a Lafette heavy tripod.
Contents page map: *Fall Weiß*, the German invasion of Poland 1939.
Contents page image: Stuka dive-bombers in action. (*Signal* magazine, public domain)

3RD ARMY
KÜCHLER
POMORZE ARMY
Torun
MODLIN ARMY
KUTNO GROUP
Plock
Kutno
Lódz
LODZ ARMY
Czestochowa
ARMY
KRAKOW ARMY
Katowice
Krakow
Tarnow
Lvov
Przemysl
CARPATHIAN ARMY

Contents

Timeline of Events

The Waffen-SS can trace its birth to March 17, 1933, when Josef "Sepp" Dietrich selected 120 men—some would say thugs—to form the Sonderkommando Berlin. Within six months the unit had grown to 800 men. On April 13, 1934, the unit became known as the Leibstandarte SS Adolf Hitler (LSSAH), by order of Heinrich Himmler. A short two months later, the LSSAH demonstrated its unwavering loyalty to Hitler during the "Night of the Long Knives," a political purge, executing some 200 Sturmabteilung (SA) senior members, including the leader Ernst Röhm, one of Hitler's oldest comrades.

In September 1934 Hitler authorized the formation of the paramilitary wing of the Nazi Party and approved the formation of the SS-Verfügungstruppe (SS-VT), a special service troop under his overall command. In 1936, Paul Hausser took over command of the SS-VT, but it was a toothless command, as power was vested with Heinrich Himmler. At the outbreak of the war the Waffen-SS comprised several subgroups: the Leibstandarte SS Adolf Hitler (LSSAH), under SS-Obergruppenführer Sepp Dietrich; the Inspectorate of Verfügungstruppe (SS-VT), under SS-Gruppenführer Paul Hausser, which comprised the Deutschland, Germania, and Der Führer regiments (the latter not yet combat-ready); the Inspectorate of Concentration Camps, under SS-Gruppenführer Theodor Eicke, which fielded four infantry and one cavalry Death's Head *Standarten*, comprising camp guards of the SS-Totenkopfverbände (SS-TV) (these Einstazgruppen troops were responsible for "police and security measures" and several "Jewish actions" in the conquered rear areas of Poland, i.e. political executions, ethnic cleansing, and genocide); and police units of Obergruppenführer und General der Polizei Kurt Daluege's Ordnungspolizei.

An SS Heimwehr Danzig NCO.

March 16, 1935: SS-Verfügungstruppe (SS-VT) is constituted, soon to be led by Paul Hausser.

January 1939: Danzig Senate President Arthur Greiser and Hitler request return of Danzig to Germany; Poland refuses.

June 1939: SS Heimwehr Danzig is formed under SS-Ostubaf. Götze.

July 25, 1939: Panzerverband Ostpreußen (aka Panzerdivision Kempf) is formed from Panzerbrigade 4, under Werner Kempf.

August 24, 1939: Molotov–Ribbentrop Pact, the Soviet–Nazi nonaggression pact, is signed.

August 31, 1939: LSSAH arrives at its assembly area on the Polish border.

September 1, 1939: German troops cut the telephone and power lines to the Polish office buildings.

September 1, 1939: *Fall Weiß*, the German invasion of Poland, begins at 0445 hours, conducted by Army Groups North (Bock) and South (Runstedt); German battleship *Schleswig-Holstein* opens fire on the Westerplatte.

September 1, 1939: LSSAH attacks Polish customs post at 0445; LSSAH in action at Boleslawice against Obrona Narodowa Polish militia.

September 1, 1939: Steiner's Deutschland Regiment in action at Mlawa.

September 3, 1939: Wisch's 1. Kompanie LSSAH in action at Raczyn. LSSAH loses first officer KIA, Franz Fischer of 3.Kp.

September 3, 1939: Panzerverband outflanks the Mlawa garrison; Steiner's Deutschland Regiment harries survivors up to Roznan, then captures Czerwin and Nordbory.

September 4 & 5, 1939: Stukas and artillery pound the Westerplatte garrison.

September 5, 1939: Dietrich is chastised by General der Artillerie Herbert Loch for poor decision-making.

September 7, 1939: Exhausted Polish garrison at Westerplatte surrenders.

September 8, 1939: XIII. Armeekorps attacks Lodz; Dietrich's troops act as a blocking force and Lodz falls.

September 10, 1939: Germania Regiment, under XXII. Armeekorps, in action at the bridgehead on the San River.

September 9–19, 1939: Polish troops conduct their only large-scale counteroffensive, along the Bzura River. Germans suffer 8,000 casualties and 4,000 POWs against the Poles' 50,000 and 170,000 POWs.

September 12–15, 1939: Kempf strikes to the southeast. The Panzerverband crosses the Bug River at Brok and engages Polish forces at Kliczym, Mink, Maz, Olwock, Siedlce, and Garwolin. The battles east of Warsaw end on September 15.

September 13, 1939: Mühlenkamp's SS-Germania motorcyclists capture 500 Polish troops trying to escape on the Przemysl–Lviv road but are forced to fall back in the afternoon in the face of a determined Polish counterattack.

September 14, 1939: Brest-Litovsk falls to Guderian's armored corps.

September 16, 1939: 4. Panzerdivision and LSSAH attack inadvertently stymies massive Polish counterattack.

September 17, 1939: The Red Army invades eastern Poland.

September 18, 1939: Exhausted by the fighting at Jaworow, SS-Germania is rested at Krakow, before being sent to Prague to integrate into the SS-Verfügungstruppe-Division.

September 19, 1939: The Poznan Army of 100,000 Polish troops surrenders to Army Group South.

September 19–28, 1939: Panzerverband in action at Modlin and Zacrozym; Witt is awarded Iron Cross 1st Class.

September 23, 1939: LSSAH subordinated to Hoth's XV. Armeekorps for the attack on the Modlin Fortress.

September 23, 1939: SS-Pionier-Bataillon comes under control of XIII. Armeekorps and 31. Infanteriedivision for the attack against Warsaw, from the southwest.

September 27, 1939: Warsaw capitulates, and 140,000 Polish troops are taken prisoner.

September 27/28, 1939: LSSAH transferred as a reserve for the Tenth Army in the Sochaczew–Bielice–Paprotnia sector.

September 29, 1939: Modlin Fortress capitulates.

October 1, 1939: Dietrich's LSSAH and Tietz's SS-Pionier-Bataillon transferred out of Poland to integrate into the SS-Verfügungstruppe-Division.

The border in 1939.

Glossary of German Military Terms

(abbreviations in brackets)

Abteilung (Abt.)	Detachment / Battalion
Allgemeine SS	General SS
Armeeabteilung	Army Detachment
Armeegruppe (AG)	Army Group
Armeekorps (AK)	Army Corps
Artillerie (Art.)	Artillery
Aufklärungs (Aufkl.)	Reconnaissance
Bataillon (Btl.)	Battalion
Batterie (Bttr.)	Battery
Einsatzgruppen	SS paramilitary death squads
Fallschirmjäger	Paratroopers
Flugabwehrkanone (Flak)	antiaircraft gun
Gebirgsjäger / Gebirgstruppe	Mountain troops
Heer	German Army
Hitlerjugend	Hitler Youth
Infanteriedivision (Inf.Div.)	Infantry Division
Kampfgruppe (KG)	Battle Group
Kavallerie (Kav.)	Cavalry
Kompanie (Kp.)	Company
Kriegsmarine	German Navy
Landser	German infantry (colloq.)
Luftwaffe	German Air Force
Nachrichtentruppe	Signal troops
Nebelwerfer (werfer)	rocket artillery
Oberkommando der Wehrmacht (OKH)	Army High Command
Oberkommando der Wehrmacht (OKW)	Armed Forces High Command
Panzerabwehrkanone (Pak)	antitank gun
Panzerfaust	man-portable antitank weapon
Panzergrenadier (Pz,Gr.)	Panzer grenadier
Panzerjäger	tank destroyer (self-propelled)
Panzerkampfwagen (Panzer)	tank / armored fighting vehicle
Panzerkorps (Pz.Korps)	Panzer Corps
Panzertruppe	Panzer troops
Pioniere	Pioneers / sappers
Schutzstaffel (SS)	lit. Protection Squadron
schwere	heavy (e.g. Tiger tank units)
Schwimmwagen	"swimming car" / light 4WD amphibious vehicle
Sonderkommando	death-camp work unit
Sonderkraftfahrzeug (Sd.Kfz.)	"special motor vehicle" / armored halftrack
SS-Hauptamt	SS Main Office
Stab	Staff
Sturmgeschütz (StuG)	assault gun
Volkssturm	National Militia / Home Guard
Waffen-SS	Armed SS
Wehrmacht	German Armed Forces

Introduction

More than 80 years ago, on September 1, 1939, World War II began. German forces invaded Poland to recover the territories lost after World War I and assigned by the victorious powers to the new Polish state. To keep their word to the Warsaw government, France and England declared war on Germany, without however implementing any military countermoves, leaving the Polish forces to defend themselves on their own, without any hope of being able to oppose the destructive power of the German blitzkrieg. Toward the middle of September, with the Polish Army routed, the Red Army too invaded Poland, under the pretext of protecting the Russian minorities in the country. It was a stab in the back, under the auspices of the Molotov–Ribbentrop Pact of the previous August. But France and England did not declare war on Stalin's USSR.

During the Polish campaign, SS fighting units participated in military operations attached to various formations of the regular army, at the specific request of the high command of the German Heer, which still considered the SS formations as parade troops, therefore unready for the front line.

The employment of SS formations during the Polish campaign was not decisive in the German victory of the forces, but on a politico-military level it was important for their definitive transformation into real fighting units. The SS units performed well, but suffered criticism from the army's high command, especially regarding the considerable number of losses suffered in proportion to the tasks assigned. Above all, the officer cadres came under attack, considered poorly and inadequately trained. The SS officers justified themselves

Leibstandarte troops drilling.

Central Europe, August 1939.

The Leibstandarte presents arms.

by, in turn, accusing the army hierarchy of the misuse of their units, often sacrificed in suicide missions. Himmler was convinced that if his units had been used independently, they would have been able to better demonstrate their full potential. Perhaps the only real fault of the SS fighters is to be found in their aggressive and unscrupulous tactics, in their bravado in launching themselves into the attack on enemy positions, and in underestimating the enemy's strength, as they had been taught during training. The battlefield experience was something else entirely. The heavy losses suffered were a useful but hard lesson that forged the fighting spirit of the soldiers of the Schutzstaffel.

This volume recounts the history of the SS fighting units in Poland, mainly the Leibstandarte Adolf Hitler, the SS-Verfügungstruppe, and the SS Heimwehr Danzig. We have therefore not dealt with the actions of other German units subordinate to SS headquarters, those engaged exclusively in rear in security tasks, such as the so-called Einsatzgruppen, involving the massacres of Polish civilians and the extermination and deportation of Jews.

German infantry on the outskirts of Warsaw.

The Danzig Question

The German claim to Danzig was the spark that ignited World War II. Current Gdansk, disputed between Germany and Poland, was for Hitler a German city, considering that in 1939, 96 percent of the inhabitants of Danzig were of Germanic origin. History also proved Hitler right: the city had belonged to the Teutonic Order from 1309 to 1454 and after a brief sojourn in the Polish kingdom, it was once again included within the borders of Prussia. The "Danzig question" arose immediately after World War I when the rulers of the resurrected Polish state demanded from the victorious Western powers an outlet to the Baltic Sea, obtaining the right to use the port of Danzig, as well as having a corridor of territory to the sea, a land corridor that physically divided East Prussia from the rest of Germany. This was a historical, geographical, and political absurdity.

The Treaty of Versailles complicated matters further, with Woodrow Wilson's "Fourteen Points" establishing an extremely ambiguous legal status for the city: Danzig was proclaimed a "free city," under the aegis of the League of Nations, but nominally under the Polish government. The official language continued to be German, the currency was the mark in the form of the Danzig *guiden*, and most of the management and government structures remained German. The free city was governed by an elective senate. Furthermore, the city had to be completely demilitarized.

A view of Danzig with its canals, 1939.

The Polish / Danzig Corridor, August 1939.

A postcard representation of the Polish Corridor and the free port of Gdansk (Danzig).

For over 10 years, relations between Danzig and the Polish state remained formally correct, until Adolf Hitler came to power in Germany in 1933, and demanded the return of the city to the Greater Reich. Over the next few years, Danzig was then transformed into a National Socialist citadel. The first SA unit in Danzig was formed as early as March 1926, but remained isolated, as there was little collaboration with the other local militias. Between 1931 and 1932, SA assault squads clashed frequently with the local communists and Social Democrats, but no firearms were ever used, only knives and other improvised weapons.

In 1935, Senate President Arthur Greiser, a fervent National Socialist, began to promulgate laws to limit the powers of the League of Nations and encouraged the construction of several military works. At the same time, starting from 1938, the Germans brought numerous volunteers disguised as tourists into the city, who were immediately placed in new military formations. In January 1939, the city's parliament and Hitler himself officially requested the return of Danzig to Germany and authorization to build a highway in the Polish corridor to connect the Reich with East Prussia. Poland naturally opposed it but declared itself willing to "discuss other means of facilitating rail and road traffic through the corridor."

Arthur Greiser.

Hitlerjugend march through Danzig, 1938.

The Polish response eliminated any other possibility of diplomatic resolution to the problem and from that moment the German generals were authorized by Hitler to prepare plans for the invasion of Poland, Plan White, or *Fall Weiß*.

August 18, 1939: Gauleiter Albert Forster reviews the troops of SS Heimwehr Danzig. On the right is SS-Ostubaf. Hans Freidemann Götze.

An SS Heimwehr Danzig soldier repositions a target on the range.

SS Heimwehr Danzig soldiers training with a light mortar, August 1939.

An SS Heimwehr Danzig artillery forward observer in training, August 1939.

Fall Weiß

The German invasion plan for Poland, codenamed *Fall Weiß*, envisaged the destruction of the Polish armed forces in the shortest possible time, with a concentric attack toward the Polish capital, brought from the southwest, from Silesia and, to the north, from Pomerania and East Prussia. Speed of execution represented an important part of the plan—due to the German general staff's concern about a possible intervention by the Allied powers alongside Poland with the consequent need to transfer troops to a Western Front to defend themselves from a possible French attack. For the new offensive, the German forces were divided into two army groups: Army Group North, under General Fedor von Bock, including the Third and Fourth Armies, and Army Group South, under General Gerd von Rundstedt, comprising the Eighth, Tenth, and Fourteenth Armies, and the Slovak army group "Bernolak."

From the northeast, from East Prussia, the Third Army of General Georg von Küchler was to attack, with the aim of reaching Warsaw from the east by joining up with General Günther von Kluge's Fourth Army, which was to strike from the northwestern border of Poland. From the west, General Walter von Reichenau's Tenth Army was to attack and carry out a pincer movement to block the bulk of the Polish forces located west of Warsaw. The flanks of von Reichenau's army would be protected by units of General Johannes Blaskowitz's Eighth Army. From the southwestern border, General Wilhelm List's Fourteenth Army was to strike and head toward the Vistula River, to cut off the retreating Polish forces.

The Danzig police in action.

Fall Weiß, the German invasion of Poland 1939.

German infantry march into Poland, September 1939.

At exactly 0445 hours on September 1, 1939, the Germans launched their armies in a grandiose encirclement maneuver, showing the entire world the efficiency of the blitzkrieg, the lightning war, based on the use of powerful, rapid strikes by motorized units, supported by aircraft. Attacking in front of the ground troops, Luftwaffe planes carried out their dual tasks of hitting targets on the ground and destroying the Polish Air Force. During the first two days of the war, Polish airfields were bombed, and any aircraft still there were destroyed.

Heavy air attacks were also launched against the road and rail networks, as well as against the main administrative and industrial centers. The superiority of the Luftwaffe over the Polish Air Force was evident from the first day of the war. On September 5, the German forces had already broken the cordon of Polish troops deployed along the border, while

The Luftwaffe over Polish territory, 1939.

Stukas attack Poland.

the Tenth Army was creating a gap in the direction of Warsaw from the south.

From September 6 to 10, German units continued their march in the direction of Warsaw. The Third and Fourth Armies of the Army Group North were pressing in the direction of the capital, while the Eighth and the Tenth Armies of Army Group South headed north, toward Warsaw and the Radom area. The attack on September 9, along the Bzura River, was the only large-scale counteroffensive carried out with any vigor by the Poles who struck at the center of the German deployment that was facing limited combat action. However, Generals Gerd von Rundstedt and Erich von Manstein, by having their forces create a diversion and bringing forward reserve troops, engaged their opponents in a difficult battle on a narrow front, beating them comprehensively. Meanwhile, elements of Army Group South were starting the assault on the Polish capital, as other Wehrmacht units continued fighting on the Bzura River. Guderian's armored corps advanced to Brest-Litovsk, which fell on September 14. These forces would soon link up with Ludwig von Kleist's armored units from the south.

On September 17, 1939, units of the Red Army, according to the terms stipulated in Molotov–Ribbentrop Pact of the previous August, in turn entered Poland from the east, putting an end to any Polish hopes. Two days later, the 100,000 men of the Poznan Army surrendered to Army Group South. Warsaw resisted for another eight days, but the campaign could already be considered over.

German tanks in Poland, 1939.

Employment of SS Units

During the Polish campaign, SS units participated in military operations attached to other formations of the German regular army, subordinate to Heer military hierarchies, who considered the SS formations still as parade troops and unready for the front line. And so, the bulk of the SS-Verfügungstruppe (Nazi Party Dispositional Troops), the Deutschland Regiment, the SS-Artillerie Standarte, the reconnaissance battalion, the antiaircraft battalion, and the signals battalion together with an army tank regiment formed a motorized division under Generalmajor Werner Kempf, former commander of Panzerbrigade 4. The unit, Panzerdivision Kempf (but also known as Panzerverband Ostpreußen), represented an experimental formation, created to verify the possibility of equipping the armored divisions with a single regiment of infantry. The Inspector General of the SS-Verfügungstruppe himself, SS-Gruppenführer Paul Hausser, was assigned to the general staff of the same unit. Panzerdivision Kempf was assigned to I. Armeekorps, Army Group North.

The SS-Standarte Germania was initially placed in reserve, assigned to the Fourteenth Army. The SS-Standarte Der Führer did not participate in the campaign as it was not fully constituted. The Leibstandarte Adolf Hitler and the SS-Pionieresturmbann were assigned to the Tenth Army.

Generalmajor Werner Kempf.

SS-Gruppenführer Paul Hausser.

German soldiers during the attack against the Polish garrison.

German troops on the Westerplatte peninsula.

The Panzerverband Ostpreußen

By order of the OKH, the staff of Panzerverband Ostpreußen (lit. East Prussia Panzer Formation) was created in Stuttgart on July 25, 1939, formed out of Panzerbrigade 4. Its command was assigned to Generalmajor Werner Kempf.

Although there was limited time available to amalgamate the various units of the division coming from the army and the SS-VT, a certain cohesion was achieved thanks to the work of General Kempf and his general staff. On August 19, the Panzerverband was attached to General Walter Petzel's I. Armeekorps, comprising 11. and 61. Infanteriedivisionen. The corps was transferred to the Osterode sector. On August 30, it prepared to cross the Polish border north of Mlawa, advancing from the Mühlen–Seewalde–Thurau–Kownath–Rontzken–Wapliz line.

A Pz.Kpfw. III of Panzerdivision Kempf in Poland, September 1939.

Command Structure of Panzerverband Ostpreußen

Div.-Kdr.: Generalmajor Kempf

Ia e O: Oberstleutnant i.G. von Bernuth

Ib: Hauptmann Billert

O2: SS-Obersturmführer Horst Geguns

Ic: SS-Hauptsturmführer Erich Grensing

IVa: Major Mertz

IVb: Oberfeldartz Dr Dalchow

Liaison staff of the SS-Verfügungstruppe

SS-Gruppenführer Hausser

SS-Sturmbannführer Ostendorff (Ia)

SS-Hauptsturmführer Klingenberg (IIa)

Panzerregiment 7: Oberst Franz Landgraf

I.Abt.: Major von Gersdorff

II.Abt.: Oberstleutnant Schmidt

SS-Rgt. Deutschland: SS-Staf. Felix Steiner

I./SS-D: SS-Sturmbannführer Schuldt

II./SS-D: SS-Ostubaf. Karl Praefcke

III./SS-D: SS-Ostubaf. Kleinheisterkamp

SS-Artillerieregiment: SS-Ostubaf. Hansen

I.Abt.: SS-Sturmbannführer Gille

II.Abt.: SS-Sturmbannführer Priess

III.Abt.: SS-Stubaf. Erspenmüller

SS-Nachr.-Abt.: SS-Sturmbannführer Weiss

SS-Aufkl.-Abt.: SS-Sturmbannführer Brandt

Panzerabwehr-Abt.511: Hauptmann La Roche

Pionier-Btl.505: Hauptmann Düllmann

2./SS-Fla-MG-Abt.: SS-Haupsturmführer Fick

Dinafü: SS-Obersturmbannführer Knapp

Sanitäts-Dienste: Oberfeldartz Dr Dalchow

SS-Verfügungstruppe (SS-VT)

The SS-Verfügungstruppe—troops at the disposal of the Führer for extraordinary purposes—was formally constituted on March 16, 1935, the date on which Hitler reestablished compulsory military service in Germany. These units, in turn, had seen their naissance in September 1934, when Hitler approved the transfer of the *Politische Bereitschaften* (political detachments) to the SS-Verfügunstruppe, or SS-VT. From these emergency political detachments, first the battalions (*Sturmbanne*) and then the regiments (*Standarten*) of the SS-Verfügungstruppe were formed. The SS-VT was to include three regiments, similar in organization to those of the Heer, each comprising three battalions, a motorcyclist company, and a mortar company. The existence of the SS-Verfügungstruppe was made public on March 16, 1935, by Hitler himself, during a speech in the Reichstag. The SS-VT, however, depended on the German army for weapons, equipment, and training, as well as for new recruits. Army officers did not like the creation of this new armed force of a political nature, above all because it remained independent of their high command and swore allegiance exclusively to Hitler. For this reason, its integration into the German military system was slow and the very formation of the SS fighting units took a back seat to the restructuring of the Wehrmacht. In 1936, Himmler appointed Paul Hausser inspector of the SS-VT with the rank of *Brigadeführer*. Hausser immediately committed himself to transforming the SS-VT into a real military force, thanks to his wealth of experience gained in the army. Starting in 1937, the SS was divided into three branches: the Allgemeine SS (the general SS), the SS-Verfügungstruppe, and the SS-Totenkopfverbände (SS-TV) for the administration of the concentration camps. On August 17, 1938, Hitler decreed that the SS military formations were neither part of the police nor the Wehrmacht but were at his disposal entirely. Only in the event of war would the SS-VT be made available to the army.

The SS Heimwehr Danzig

In October 1938, the III. Bataillon of the SS-Totenkopfdstandarte 4 Ostmark was formed in Berlin, under SS-Obersturmbannführer Hans-Freidemann Götze. Himmler decreed that this unit would serve as the nucleus of a local defense force in Danzig. In June 1939, the Senate of the free city of Danzig voted to create a city defense force (*Heimwehr*). Himmler supported its formation, secretly providing volunteers from SS formations: the entire III. Bataillon Götze, together with the SS-Totenkopf-PanzerAbwehr-Ersatz-Sturm, which was the antitank training company of the Totenkopfstandarte. The SS soldiers arrived in the city disguised as tourists so as not to alarm Allied spies and above all the Polish authorities.

Reinforced by 500 volunteers recruited in Danzig itself, the Heimwehr Danzig (lit. Danzig Home Defense) was officially classified as an SS formation with around 1,550 men and

An antitank squad of the SS Heimwehr Danzig.

An ADGZ armored car of the SS Heimwehr Danzig, followed by some members of the unit, heads towards the area of the Polish Post Office in Danzig, September 1, 1939.

SS Heimwehr Danzig units on the Oxhofter Kampe, the Oxhofter headland.

placed under Götze himself, promoted on the eve of the war to the rank of *Standartenführer*. The unit was structured as a reinforced infantry battalion, with four rifle companies, a machine-gun company, an artillery company, two antitank companies, a pioneer platoon, a signals platoon, and a transport company.

An antitank unit of SS Heimwehr Danzig engaged in the Polish campaign, 1939.

In Profile:
Hans-Friedemann Götze (1897–1940)

Hans-Friedemann Götze, son of SS-Brigadeführer Friedemann Götze, was born on November 3, 1897, in Rendsburg, Schleswig-Holstein, SS-Nr. 281 771. He saw service in World War I and was awarded the Honor Cross of the World War 1914/1918. Between December 1937 and March 1938, he was employed as an instructor officer at the SS-Junkerschule Bad Tölz. On September 1, 1939, he was promoted to the rank of SS-Standartenführer, commanding the SS Heimwehr Danzig. Some 1,550 members of his unit participated in an attack on the Polish Post Office in Danzig on September 1, 1939. A week later, the SS Heimwehr Danzig massacred 33 Polish civilians in the village of Ksiazki. On May 27, 1940, while leading 3. SS-Panzerdivision Totenkopf in the Pas-de-Calais, Götze was shot and killed in the village of Paradis by a British sniper from the 2nd Battalion Royal Norfolk Regiment. Later that day, 97 captured members of the Norfolk Regiment were executed by the Totenkopf in what became known as Le Paradis massacre. Götze was recipient of the Iron Cross First and Second Class, the Baltic Cross, Reichs Sport Badge in Gold, Clasp to the Iron Cross Second Class, Horseman's Badge in Bronze, and the Danzig Cross, 1st and 2nd Class.

August 18, 1939: Gauleiter Albert Forster hands over the official banner of the SS Heimwehr Danzig to its commander SS-Ostubaf. Götze.

SS Heimwehr Danzig Senior Commanders

Kommandeur: SS-Ostubaf. Götze

Stabs.Kompanie: SS-Ostubaf. Götze

Adjutant: SS-Ostuf. Westermann

Chef d. Stab: SS-Hstuf. Sparmann

I.Schützenkompanie: SS-Hstuf. Karl Thier

II.Sch.Kp.: SS-Ostuf. Willy Bredemeier

III.Sch.Kp.: SS-Hstuf. Georg Braun

IV.Sch.Kp.: SS-Hstuf. Erich Urbanitz

V.Sch.Kp.: SS-Hstuf. Otto Baier

13.Inf.Gesch.Kp.: SS-Hstuf. Schulz

14.Pz.Abw.Kp.: SS-HStuf. Josef Steiner

15.Pz.Abw.Kp.: SS-Ostuf. Otto Leiner

Kdr Pi.Zug: SS-Ustuf. Knaack

Kdr Nach.Zug: SS-Ustuf. Stieglitz

Kdr Trans.Kp.: SS-Ostuf. Schneider

Ufficiali medici: SS-Hstuf. Dr Kamholz, SS-Hstuf. Dr Wertschitzsky

Gruppe Eberhardt

In June 1939, again in Danzig, another SS unit, the SS-Wachsturmbann Eimann, was formed under Sturmbannführer Kurt Eimann. This formation was to serve as an armed reserve for the Danzinger SS-Standarte 36 but was also to be used in the territories of the Polish Corridor to convince *Volksdeutschen* to enlist in the Allgemeine SS, the Totenkopfverbände, and the Heimwehr Danzig itself.

On the eve of war, the SS and German police units in Danzig were grouped into the Gruppe Eberhardt, under Generalleutnant Friedrich-Georg Eberhardt, head of the Danzig Police. These units were the Landespolizei Regiment, Kustenschütz der Danziger Polizei, SS Heimwehr Danzig, and SS-Wachsturmbann Eimann.

Generalmajor Friedrich-Georg Eberhardt.

The Attack Begins

At 0445 hours, on September 1, 1939, German forces attacked. The war, however, had already begun half an hour earlier in Danzig, exactly at 0417 hours, when members of the SS Heimwehr Danzig, after having received the codeword "*Dora*," together with other German units, surrounded the Polish Post Office, demanding its surrender. The postal workers, all armed and already alerted to any eventuality, responded by opening fire. At the same time, in the city's port, the German battleship *Schleswig-Holstein* opened fire against the port fortifications and against the Westerplatte, an old fortress north of Gdansk, as well as an ammunition depot manned by Polish forces. "Danzig is in German hands, it has once again become part of the Third Reich," Gauleiter Albert Forster proclaimed on the radio. At the same time, 5. Kompanie SS Heimwehr Danzig, under SS-Hstuf. Baier, was engaged at Dirschau, taking a bridge over the Vistula River.

The entrance to the port of Gdansk, 1939. On the right, the Westerplatte peninsula.

German motorized troops in a Polish village.

A German mortar in action.

The Attack on the Polish Post Office

The Polish Post Office in Danzig was created in 1919, under the Treaty of Versailles. Its buildings were to be regarded as Polish extraterritorial property. In 1930, the "Gdansk 1" building on Helvetiusplatz in the old city became the main Polish Post Office, with a direct telephone line to Poland. In 1939, approximately 100 employees served in the office. Many of them were part of Polish paramilitary organizations and were responsible for the safety of personnel. As relations with Germany became increasingly strained, the Polish high command moved a reserve officer, Konrad Guderski, into the office, tasking him with organizing the defenses around Polish buildings. At 0400 on September 1, 1939, the Germans cut the telephone and power lines to the Polish office buildings.

When the battleship *Schleswig-Holstein* began opening fire, the assault on the post office also began. The German units involved in the attack included special units of the Danzig Police and SS units, such as the SS Heimwehr Danzig and the Wachsturmbann "E." The SS Heimwehr Danzig units counted on the support of some Austrian ADGZ armored cars, on which they had painted the skull and double runes. Each vehicle was named after German provinces, such as Ostmark and Sudentenland. Field operations were led by German Police Colonel Willi Bethke. The first German assault, launched head-on, was repelled. The Germans attempted to force the main entrance of the building without success.

A second attack carried out on the flanks was again repelled, but during this second firefight, the Polish commander Konrad Guderski was killed. Around 1100, the Germans sent two 7.5-cm artillery pieces to the scene, which immediately began pounding the Polish

German soldiers and policemen near the post office.

German soldiers during the attack on the post office.

defenses. However, despite this artillery support, a fresh assault was still repelled. At around 1500, the Germans announced a two-hour truce, simultaneously demanding a Polish surrender. Having received a negative response from the Poles, they resumed the attack while a 10.5-cm artillery piece and an engineering unit arrived on site and began placing explosive charges around the building. At around 1700, a charge of around 600 kilograms of explosives was detonated, causing part of the wall around the post office to collapse. Immediately afterward, some German pioneers went into action with flamethrowers, and it was at that point that the Poles raised the white flag.

SS Heimwehr Danzig soldiers take shelter behind an ADGZ armored car during the attack on the post office.

Armored cars and members of SS Heimwehr Danzig engaged in the attack on the post office.

The entrance to the Polish Post Office destroyed.

The final moment of the attack and the explosion.

The defenders of the Polish Post Office captured at the end of the battle, escorted by members of SS Heimwehr Danzig.

The Attack Against the Westerplatte

The Westerplatte fortress was assigned to the Poles to secure and safeguard their interests in the port of Gdansk. In 1925, the League of Nations authorized Poland to maintain a garrison of 88 soldiers in the fortress. In 1939, their numbers rose to 182 men. The heavy armament included a 7.5-cm artillery piece, two 3.7-cm antitank guns, four mortars, and some medium-caliber machine guns. There were no real fortifications, just a few bunkers hidden in the forest on the peninsula. The Polish garrison was separated from Danzig by a port canal and was connected to the mainland only by a narrow quay. In command of

Gustav Kleikamp.

The *Schleswig Holstein* opens fire on Westerplatte.

The Westerplatte under German fire.

the garrison was Major Henryk Sucharski, who was replaced on September 2 by Captain Franciszek Dabrowski. On August 25, 1939, the German battleship *Schleswig-Holstein* officially arrived in Danzig on a courtesy visit. The battleship dropped anchor in the canal to the right of the Westerplatte. During the *Schleswig-Holstein*'s presence in Danzig waters, the Polish Westerplatte garrison was on alert 24 hours a day. On board the ship, below deck, was an entire assault company of naval infantry of 225 men, the Marinestosstruppkompanie, under Oberleutnant Wilhelm Henningsen.

At 0445, on September 1, 1939, the commander of the German battleship, Kapitän zur See Gustav Kleikamp, gave the order to open fire on the Polish garrison, with its 18 guns of calibers varying between 8.8 and 28 cm. The bombing of the peninsula lasted for about an hour. When the guns stopped firing, the ground attack began, led by Henningsen's naval assault company and SS Heimwehr Danzig units, which had arrived on site. The Polish

German troops during the attack on the peninsula.

soldiers, stationed along the perimeter walls of the fortress, responded with machine guns and mortars, causing serious losses to the attackers.

The German forces returned to attack several more times during the day, suffering further losses and without any concrete results. On September 2, a white flag was spotted on the Westerplatte, but it was only a trap set by the Poles: when the German troops tried to approach the garrison, they again came under enemy fire, suffering yet further losses. For the rest of the day, the fortress was subjected to a massive fresh bombardment by naval artillery and for the first time by Stuka dive-bombers. A bunker with seven Polish soldiers and a machine gun inside was completely blown up. During the following night of September 3/4, two new assaults by marine infantry were unsuccessfully attempted.

During September 4 and 5, artillery bombardments and attacks from the air by the Stukas continued. The Poles, now exhausted, without water, without supplies of any kind and aware that no one was coming to rescue them, nevertheless decided to continue resisting. In addition to the German naval batteries, an 8.8-cm gun battery located at Heubude, two destroyers anchored at Brosen, two 21-cm mortar batteries, and a coastal battery at Glettkau renewed the shelling. The bombings continued during the morning of September 6, while in the afternoon the ground attacks resumed, but were once again repelled.

At dawn on September 7, the German infantry attacked again. The exhausted Polish soldiers, without hope, almost all wounded, finally decided to surrender. After seven days of incessant fighting, all Polish defensive positions on the Westerplatte peninsula were captured. SS Heimwehr Danzig units alone reported the loss of around 50 men, dead and wounded.

Members of the Marinestosstruppkompanie on board.

Employment in Other Sectors

Once Danzig was conquered, SS Heimwehr Danzig units continued to be involved along the coast northwest of the city, in collaboration with the army units, in destroying pockets of Polish resistance. Starting on September 8, 1939, some companies were engaged in heavy fighting along the coastal area known as Oxhofter Kampe, where several Polish fortifications were installed. The clashes here lasted until September 19. Immediately afterward, the entire unit was engaged in the occupation of the port city of Gdynia, 16 kilometers northwest of Danzig. Here too, the Germans encountered strong resistance from the Polish troops. In this period, SS Heimwehr Danzig was placed under the Pomeranian Local Defense Division, under Oberst Graf von Rittberg.

In war bulletins the SS unit was in fact mentioned as the "Bataillon Rittberg" and this sent Himmler into apoplexy, in constant conflict as he was with the high command of the Heer. Until the end of the Polish campaign, SS Heimwehr Danzig units continued operating

Hitler greets his triumphant troops, 1939.

Two members of Hitler's SS escort battalion in Poland.

in Pomerania and in the Polish Corridor, where they were mainly engaged in mopping-up operations to flush out the last groups of Polish soldiers still resisting, and to eliminate the snipers.

Once the Polish campaign was over, the SS Heimwehr Danzig was disbanded, and its elements incorporated into the new SS division, Totenkopf. In particular, the Heimwehr veterans were mainly placed in the artillery regiment and in the SS-Totenkopf-Infanterieregiment 3 (mot.), under SS-Staf. Götze.

SS-Deutschland soldiers.

Soldiers of the SS Heimwehr Danzig with two captured Polish snipers, September 1939.

Reichsführer-SS Heinrich Himmler inspects Heimwehr Danzig units in Gotenhafen, September 1939.

Employment of the Other Totenkopf Units

At the beginning of September 1939, the SS-Totenkopfstandarte Oberbayern under SS-Ostubaf. Max Simon, SS-Totenkopfstandarte Brandenburg under SS-Staf. Paul Nostitz, and SS-Totenkopfstandarte Thuringen under SS-Stubaf. Heimo Hierthes, left their headquarters in Dachau, Sachsenhausen, and Buchenwald respectively, for deployment to Poland. Hitler himself had ordered the deployment of the three Totenkopf regiments in the rear area of the Polish front, to engage in police and security actions. Their military use was not decisive in the German victory, but on a political-military level it was important for their definitive establishment as fighting units. The Totenkopf units were engaged in mopping-up actions in Polish territory, destroying enemy stragglers and terrorizing the civilian population. The SS-Totenkopfstandarte Oberbayern and SS-Totenkopfstandarte Thuringen were transferred to the rear of the operational area of the German Tenth Army, operating between northern Silesia and the Vistula River, south of Warsaw. The SS-Totenkopfstandarte Brandenburg instead followed General Blaskowitz's Eighth Army, operating in the Poznan area and central–western Poland. Theodor Eicke did not personally accompany his units in the field but directed them from Hitler's special train (*Führersonderzug*) with the post of *Höhere SS und Polizei Führer* (HSSuPF) (High Commander of the Police and SS) for the regions conquered by the Eighth and Tenth Armies.

Max Simon was born on January 6, 1899, in Breslau, SS-Nr. 83 086. During World War I, he participated as a private in the fighting in Macedonia, and subsequently fought on the Western Front, where he was decorated with the Iron Cross Second Class. At the end of the war, in 1919, he joined the Silesian Freikorps. His unit was later incorporated into the Reichswehr as the 16. Kavallerieregiment and Simon was promoted to *Unterfeldwebel*. In May 1933 he joined the SS and was assigned to SS-Standarte 47 in Gera. In November 1934, he was promoted to *Untersturmführer*. In 1935 he enlisted with the SS-Totenkopfstandarte Oberbayern. In 1937, with the rank of *Sturmbannführer*, he obtained command of the I./Sta. Oberbayern.

Paul Nostitz was born March 25, 1892, in Lyck, East Prussia, SS-Nr. 32 617. He had previously served as *Stabsführer* SS-Abschnitt XXXX (SS-Section XXXX), commanding SS-Standarte 35 in Kassel and SS-Totenkopfstandarte Thüringen.

Heimo Hierthes was born July 25, 1897, in Neubeurg a.d. Donau, SS-Nr. 282 042.

In Profile:
SS Armored Cars in Poland, September 1939

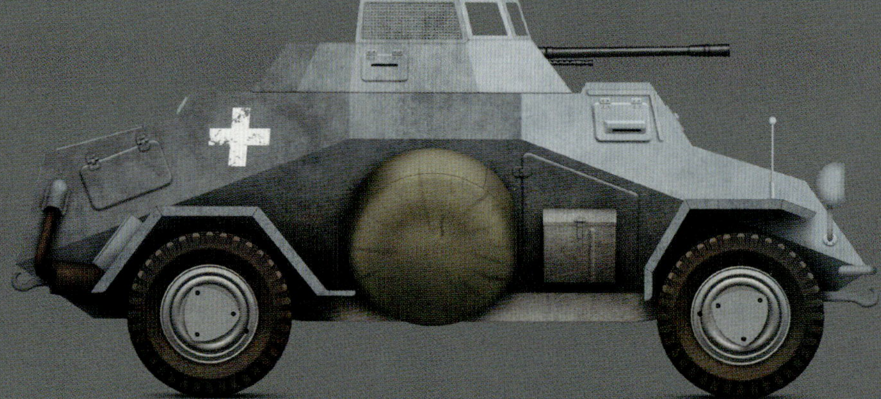

Sd.Kfz. 222 (4x4) armored car of the SS-Standarte (motorisiert) "LAH," Poland, September 1939. (Battlefield Design)

Sd.Kfz. 232 (8x8) armored car of the SS-Standarte (motorisiert) "LAH," Poland, September 1939. (Battlefield Design)

Austro-Daimler ADGZ (8x8) named *Ostmark*, armoured car attached to the SS Heimwehr Danzig, Danzig (Gdansk), September 1, 1939. (Battlefield Design)

Leibstandarte Adolf Hitler in Action

SS-Ogruf. Sepp Dietrich.

While the winds of war were blowing and diplomatic efforts were at work to calm them, the Leibstandarte Adolf Hitler reorganized its units during that hot summer of 1939. At the end of June, new changes of command occurred thanks to the arrival of officers from other SS-VT units. SS-Staf. Wilhelm Bittrich was appointed *Oberst beim Stabe*, and SS-Ostubaf. Carl Reichsritter von Oberkamp took command of II./LSSAH. In the same battalion, SS-Ostuf. Otto Baum took over the command of 7. Kompanie and SS-Ostuf. Hans Bissinger 9. Kompanie. The main changes regarding weapons and equipment affected the heavy companies, which in addition to the machine guns, also comprised a mortar platoon that included six medium 8.1-cm mortars (m.Gr.W.34). On August 25, the regiment was put on standby for the upcoming campaign against Poland: at 0400 it set off in the direction of Hunsfeld, passing through Luckau, Trebnitz, Breslau, Kunesdorf, Weigelsdorf, and Wildschütz.

Leibstandarte troops on the march.

SS-Hstuf. Wilhelm Bittrich.

Wilhelm Bittrich was born February 26, 1894, in Wernigerode im Harz. In 1932 he joined the SS, SS-Nr. 39 177, as part of the SS-Fliegerstaffel Ost (SS Flying Echelon East). He later gained command of SS-Standarte 74, before leaving the Allgemeine SS in August 1934 to take command of the second company of SS-Standarte Germania. In October 1936, he was transferred to the Deutschland Regiment as commander of II. Bataillon, a position he held until the summer of 1938. In June 1939 Bittrich was transferred to the Leibstandarte as an adjutant on Sepp Dietrich's general staff, where he remained until at the end of the Polish campaign.

Karl Ferdinand Reichsritter von Oberkamp was born in Munich on October 30, 1893, SS-Nr. 310 306. He distinguished himself during World War I on the Lorraine front between 1914–1915 and subsequently in the Tyrol in the Alpenkorps, in Verdun in 1916, and in the Carpathians in 1917. He ended the war as commander of 14. Kompanie Jägerregiment 3. He served in the Frankish Corps Oberland between 1920 and 1923 and participated in the failed Munich Putsch of 1923. He then began work as a physical education teacher and only in March 1935 did he join the Reichswehr, where he exploited his past in the Alpenkorps, first as *Major beim Stab* of the Geb.Jg.Rgt. 98 and then as Adjutant in the 3.Geb.Div. in 1938. On November 1, 1938, he entered the SS with the rank of *SS-Sturmbannführer*, as a tactics instructor at the SS-Junkerschule.

SS-Ustuf. Otto Baum.

Otto Baum was born November 15, 1911, in Hechingen-Stetten. In 1933 he joined the SS, SS-Nr. 237 056. He was immediately transferred to the SS-Junkerschule Braunschweig. Promoted to *Untersturmführer* on April 20, 1936, he took command of a platoon of the Germania Regiment at Arolsen, before being transferred two years later to the Standarte Der Führer, created in May 1938 in Austria, in command of 10. Kompanie.

Hans Bissinger was born January 25, 1913, in Munich, SS-Nr. 53 698. Previously he had served in the 2./Sta. Deutschland.

Heinz Bertling was born October 20, 1898, in Kiel, SS-Nr. 60 258. He joined the SS on April 1, 1931. On March 12, 1934, he was promoted to the rank of *SS-Untersturmführer* serving on the General Staff of the SS-Abschnitt XXVI. He left the SS that same year to move to the Landespolizei with the rank of *Hauptmann*. He returned to the SS in March 1935 as a professor of tactics at the SS-Junkerschule Braunschweig. Between February and April 1938, he served in the SS-Totenkopf-Standarte 3. Before moving to the Leibstandarte, he provisionally commanded the I./Sta. Deutschland.

SS soldiers in musketry training.

On August 26, the formation of a depot battalion for the Leibstandarte, the Ersatz-Bataillon LSSAH, was constituted, to provide replacements for any losses the unit suffered in combat. The new unit was placed under SS-Ostubaf. Heinz Bertling.

During the late afternoon of August 25, 1939, the SS units arrived east of Breslau, where they were placed under the control of the XIII. Armeekorps of the General der Kavallerie Maximilian Reichsfreiherr von Weichs, who ordered their transfer to the Glausche–Kunzendorf–Schönau–Essdorf sector and to the forests south of Bernstadt.

The offensive was scheduled to begin the next day at 0430 hours. For this purpose, the II./Art.Rgt.46 (Major Krix) had been attached to the Leibstandarte, to provide artillery support. At 2200 the units set off, but when they reached the halfway mark, around midnight, the order to stop arrived: the offensive had been postponed for a few days pending possible diplomatic developments. On the 26th, around midday, a new transfer order arrived for the Namslau–Pangau–Bernstadt–Prietzen–Windisch–Marchwitz sector, due to the failure of the 30. Infanteriedivision to arrive at the Eighth Army assembly area.

German armored cars advance into Polish territory.

LSSAH Senior Commanders, August 31, 1939

Rgt.-Kdr.: SS-Obergruppenführer Dietrich
Oberst beim Stabe: SS-Standartenführer Bittrich
Adjutant: SS-Hauptsturmführer Collani
Quartiermeister: SS-Hauptsturmführer Ewert
Ordonnanz-Offizier: SS-Untersturmführer Maas
Verwaltungs-Offizier: SS-Ostubaf. Clemens, poi SS-Hstuf. Bludau
Rgt.-Arzt: SS-Hauptsturmführer Dr Wille
Rgt.-Ingenieur: SS-Hauptsturmführer Scheide
Rgt.-Nachr.-Zug: SS-Obersturmführer Keilhaus
Rgt.-Kradmelde-Zug: SS-Ostuf. Georg Sandkühler
Musik-Zug: SS-Hauptsturmführer Müller-John

I.Btl.-Kdr.: SS-Obersturmbannführer Kohlroser
Adjutant: SS-Ustuf. Walter Malinowski
Ord.-Offz.: SS-Untersturmführer Janssen
Verw.-Offz.: SS-Hauptsturmführer Wittesch
Abt.-Arzt: SS-Hauptsturmführer Dr Schulz
TFK: SS-Hauptsturmführer Gross
TFW: SS-Hstuf. Schröter, then SS-Ustuf. Schürer
1.Kp.: SS-Hauptsturmführer Wisch
2.Kp.: SS-Hstuf. Ernst Meyer-Andresen
3.Kp.: SS-Ostuf. Fischer, poi SS-Ostuf. Wichmann
4.(MG)Kp.: SS-Hauptsturmführer Bestmann

II.Btl.-Kdr.: SS-Ostubaf. von Oberkamp
Adjutant: SS-Obersturmführer Klingemeier
Verw.-Offz.: SS-Hauptsturmführer Bludau
Abt.-Arzt: SS-Hauptsturmführer Dr Rick
TFK: SS-Obersturmführer Stoltz
TFW: SS-Hauptsturmführer Nowak
5.Kp.: SS-Hauptsturmführer Mohnke
6.Kp.: SS-Hauptsturmführer Rudolf Lange
7.Kp.: SS-Hauptsturmführer Baum
8.(MG)Kp.: SS-Stuf. Otto Dieterichs, then SS-Hstuf. August Dieterichs

III.Btl.-Kdr. : SS-Ostubaf. Trabandt
Adjutant: SS-Obersturmführer von Stein
Ord.-Offz.: SS-Untersturmführer Bremer
Verw.-Offz. : SS-Hauptsturmführer Sucker
Abt.-Arzt: SS-Hauptsturmführer Dr Jatzlauk
TFK: SS-Obersturmführer Stoltz
9.Kp.: SS-Hauptsturmführer Hans Bissinger
10.Kp.: SS-Hauptsturmführer Polewacz
11.Kp.: SS-Hauptsturmführer Marks
12.(MG)Kp.: SS-Hstuf. Garthe
13.(IG)Kp.: SS-Hauptsturmführer Mallé
14.(Pz.Jg.)Kp.: SS-Hstuf. Meyer
15.(Kradsch.)Kp.: SS-Hstuf. Hofmann
Panzerspäh-Zug: SS-Ostuf. Schönberger
Pionier-Zug: SS-Ostuf. Hansen
Leichte-Inf.-Kol.: SS-Ostuf. Siebken

In Profile:
Hubert Meyer (1913–2012)

Hubert Meyer was born in Berlin on December 5, 1913, and joined the SS-VT on July 15, 1933, SS-Nr. 266 464. He was assigned to 12. Kompanie of the SS-Standarte Deutschland on August 4, 1934. In 1936 he was selected and admitted to the SS-Junkerschule in Bad Tölz, followed by a course for platoon leaders. On April 20, 1937, he was promoted to the rank of *SS-Untersturmführer*. On May 1, 1937 he obtained command of a platoon of the 10. Kompanie LSSAH. In November 1938, he was promoted to *SS-Obersturmführer* and led his platoon in the Polish campaign, receiving the Iron Cross Second Class on November 8, 1939. He took part in the invasion of the Low Countries, the invasion of France, and in Operation *Barbarossa*. In February 1943, he commanded a regiment at the Third Battle of Kharkov, and was awarded the German Cross in Gold on May 6, 1943. In September 1943 Meyer graduated from the General Staff Officer course and was assigned to the 12. SS-Panzerdivision Hitlerjugend, which he commanded following divisional commander Kurt Meyer's capture, until October 24, 1944. After the war, Meyer was active in HIAG (Hilfsgemeinschaft auf Gegenseitigkeit der Angehörigen der ehemaligen Waffen-SS, lit. Mutual aid association of former Waffen-SS members), a denialist Waffen-SS lobby group and was its last president before the organization was dissolved in 1992. In 1982, his book *Kriegsgeschichte der 12 SS-Panzerdivision Hitlerjugend* was published to some acclaim by Munin Verlag (later in English as *The History of the 12. SS-Panzerdivision Hitlerjugend*). He was 98 when he died.

SS-Ostuf. Hubert Meyer.

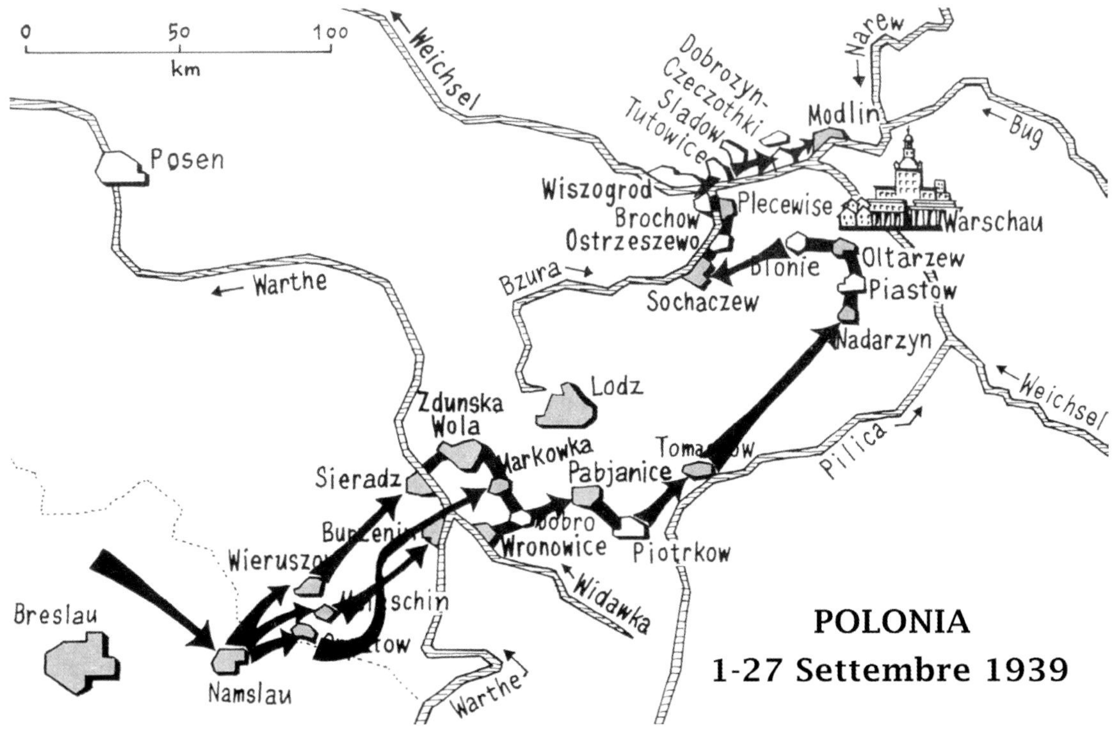

A contemporary postcard of the Leibstandarte deployments in Poland between September 1–27, 1939.

A Leibstandarte Sd.Kfz. 231 armored car hit and abandoned by its crew.

Leibstandarte soldiers in Polish territory.

A Leibstandarte Sd.Kfz. 232 armored car advances into Polish territory, September 1939.

German motorcycle scouts in Poland, 1939.

The Leibstandarte set off by dividing its units into four groups. For the start of the offensive, its use had in the meantime been clarified: taking advantage of its mobility, being a motorized unit, it was to move to the sector east of Kronstadt,[1] and from there, it was to advance on the Droschkau–Trembatschau line and subsequently seize the city of Wieruszow, the first real objective of the attack. The SS regiment was then to continue toward Zdunska Wola, secure and defend the passages over the Warta River (Warthe in German) by establishing a bridgehead on the Monice–Kol.Podlezice–Mecke Wola–Mnichow–Chalupia–Mala line. Even though it was motorized, and much emphasis was placed on its mobility, the Leibstandarte was nevertheless assigned a "sandy" route, while the only truly passable road in the sector was assigned to the 17. Infanteriedivision. After four days of waiting, on August 31, the march order finally arrived and around 1900, the vanguard of the Leibstandarte began moving toward the Polish border.

It arrived at its assembly area, in the Alteichen sector, during the night. Here, further details of its mission arrived: Sepp Dietrich's units were to capture the bridge at Gola, with a surprise attack, and crossings were to be opened over the Prosna River at Boleslawice, Wieruszow, and Weglewice. Once these bridges had been taken, the SS units were to wait for the vanguards of the 10. Infanteriedivision and the 17. Infanteriedivision.

1 Gen.Kdo.XIII.AK, Tagesbefehl v.26.8.1939.

Albert Frey was born February 16, 1913, in Heidelberg, SS-Nr. 111 913. Before moving to the Leibstandarte, he served in the Standarte Deutschland and attended the SS-Junkerschule Braunschweig.

Kurt Meyer was born in Jerxheim, near Braunschweig, December 23, 1910. After having attended elementary school, Meyer began business studies but had to interrupt them to assist with his family's economic crisis. He then began work at a factory and during 1928–1929 worked in a mine. In October 1929 he was able to enlist in the Mecklenburg police force. On October 15, 1931, he was accepted into the SS, SS-Nr.17 559, in 22. SS-Standarte Schwerin. On May 15, 1934, he was transferred to Hitler's bodyguard, the Leibstandarte SS Adolf Hitler, with the rank of *SS-Untersturmführer*. In September 1936 he was promoted to the rank of *SS-Obersturmführer* and took command of 14.(Pz.Jg.)Kp. On September 12, 1937, he was promoted to *Hauptsturmführer*.

Kurt Meyer.

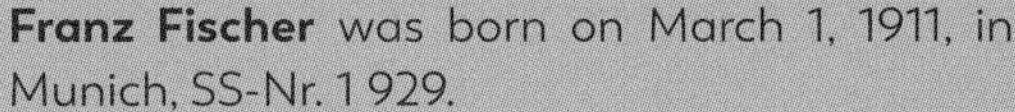

Franz Fischer was born on March 1, 1911, in Munich, SS-Nr. 1 929.

Early Clashes

At 0445, on September 1, 1939, the Leibstandarte engaged in battle. An infantry support gun from the 13. (IG) Kompanie opened fire on the Polish customs post while an assault unit—including armored cars, a motorcycle platoon, and a platoon from 9. Kompanie—seized the bridge over the Prosna River, near Gola, in a coup de main. SS-Ostuf. Frey, *Zugführer* (platoon leader) of 9. Kompanie, described those early battles:

> In the Polish area, at the entrance to the bridge, there was a small guard post where, according to the testimonies of the local inhabitants, there was an electric detonator that controlled the explosive charges placed under the same bridge. As I crossed it, I ordered the machine gun to fire at the guard post to prevent anyone from approaching the detonator. A uniformed soldier was later found dead near the scene. After crossing the bridge, the motorcyclists continued in the direction of the villages of Gola and Chroscin, through the forests, with the threat of enemy snipers well hidden in the forest.

SS-Uscha. Bröll, also a *Zugführer*, reported:

> In the center of the village, we were very surprised by the intensity of the enemy fire, coming from every direction: from the houses, from the trees, everywhere there were enemy nests that we could barely detect. It was an important lesson for me in how to employ a platoon in the vanguard. Fortunately, at that moment there was a great distance between the rearguard forces, but in any case, it was difficult to organize the various scattered elements that had spread out, put them under cover and put the vehicles in a safe place.

At 0920, the village of Boleslawice was taken after street battles and the loss of two armored cars, hit by enemy antitank guns. Meanwhile, 10. Kompanie LSSAH, reinforced by a platoon of armored cars and two groups of motorcyclists, was deployed on the right flank.

The commander of his vanguard, SS-Ostuf. Hubert Meyer, recounted the advance of his unit:

> While the bulk of the battalion continued toward Boleslawice, 10. Kompanie was busy covering the right flank passing through the village of Wojcin. My platoon formed the vanguard of the company while a scouting patrol continued farther ahead at the limit of our vision. The houses along the Prosna crossing appeared deserted; only chickens could be seen, terrified by the explosions. Our weapons were ready to fire as we moved up both sides of the sandy village road. We thought that the civilians were behind the closed windows, full of resentment toward us. Thus, we approached the second village. At the entrance to Wojcin, about two kilometers farther away, the road curved sharply to the right. The lead patrol disappeared from our sight just as shots came from the village. I rushed to take cover in the nearest houses with my men. One of them, Sturmmann Herlitze, was lying in the ditch along the road and moaning terribly. The other men had set up on the left of the road, where there were no houses, in a potato field. We were surprised that the shooting did not stop and that we could not identify where the firing was coming from. I ordered two of my men to take the wounded man to a house while I moved forward a few houses to get a clearer idea of the situation.

SS-Hstuf. Kurt Meyer.

SS-Hstuf. Wilhelm Mohnke.

> The enemy fire continued, and a bullet hit a wall or a roof tile: no one dared cross the road or even move. Our advance had been blocked. Although disappointed, I focused on the mission and regained my composure. I was thus able to determine that the shots were coming from pistols and rifles hidden in a corner of a house on our left. I ordered the men under cover in the field to open fire on the roofs, trees, and houses located in front of them to allow the main platoon to advance through the gardens at the back of the houses. I gave the order to the lead unit to proceed. It did so, but timidly: we were no longer in a training session. There was nothing left for me to do but put myself at the head of the platoon. At that moment, enemy the fire intensified, but after leaping forward, the men followed me without question. Running quickly, we reached the perpendicular road and the firing stopped. It was clear that the shooters were armed civilians. The threat had been removed: we had demonstrated that not all bullets found their target. Herlitze, our wounded comrade, was transported to the field hospital where he died during the night due to his head wound.

On one point, however, Meyer was wrong. The shooters were not armed civilians, but members of the Obrona Narodowa (National Defense), an armed militia formed from territorials. The leading elements of the Leibstandarte continued to fight until 1300. On the right flank, 10. Kompanie LSSAH passed the village of Wojcin and continued to advance north toward Wiewiorka and the woods located east of Mieleszyn. While on the left flank, the main body of the III./LSSAH passed through the villages of Boleslawice, Chotynin, Piaski, and Kamionka until reaching a line that ran from Podjaworek to the northern outskirts of Kamionka. The battalion was blocked by enemy fire coming from the heights of the Sokolniki Forest and from Mieleszyn.

Thanks to the precise and effective support fire of the II./Art.Rgt.46 batteries, the enemy positions were overwhelmed by the SS around 1530. The advance was thus able to resume, bringing Dietrich's men to the eastern area of Wieruszow. In the evening, a patrol was sent toward the railway line to establish a connection with units of the 17. Infanteriedivision, in the direction of Wieruszow itself.

In the words of Kurt Meyer, the description of the morale of the men during this first day of war:

> The darkness that descended masked the destruction of the day. The disaster on the battlefield was now visible through the fires around us whose living flames rose high into the sky. The horizon was marked by burning villages and a thick blanket

SS-Hstuf. Teddy Wisch.

SS-Ostubaf. Martin Kohlroser.

> of smoke billowed above the wounded earth. We sat in silence behind the remains of a wall, and we looked at the smoking remains of what must have been a farm.

All the objectives had been achieved, mainly due to limited enemy forces present in the sector. The Poles had only deployed a few border guard units reinforced by Obrona Narodowa militiamen. Their mission was to delay the German advance as much as possible while waiting for the arrival of the 19th Polish Infantry Division and a cavalry brigade, engaged east of Wieruszow. The next day, the Leibstandarte was transferred to 17. Infanteriedivision, to cover the right flank of the corps. This time the II./LSSAH of SS-Hstuf. Wilhelm Mohnke moved forward: the positions of Mieleszyn, Podjaworek, and Jaworek were quickly overcome, while only near the village of Parcice was it necessary to fight to open the way.

The 6. Kompanie LSSAH then moved to the vanguard, finding itself facing the Polish cavalry units who were desperately trying to block the German advance. At around 1500, the SS company managed to get as far as the Lyskornia crossroads, so a reconnaissance patrol was immediately sent in the direction of Wilichnowy to establish contact with the 17. Infanteriedivision. At the same time, a linkup on the right with the units of the 13. Infanteriedivision was also effected.

In the late afternoon, fresh fighting broke out around the villages of Biala and Biala Rzadowa, the capture of which was made possible thanks to the support fire of the II./Art. Rgt.46. On September 3, the I./LSSAH took the lead, with orders to pass through the villages of Raczyn, Czarnozyly, Dabrowa Miekka, Stolec, and Niechmirow. At the vanguard was the LSSAH's 1. Kompanie of SS-Hstuf. Teddy Wisch, the most prestigious company of the SS.

On that day, September 3, Wisch's men had to fight inside Raczyn to open the way, against elements of two Polish regiments. In the end the entire battalion had to intervene to push the enemy back. During the bloody fighting, the Leibstandarte suffered its first fallen officer, SS-Ostuf. Franz Fischer, commander of 3. Kompanie. SS-Ostubaf. Kohlroser wasted no time and launched his unit in pursuit of the enemy, however the sandy roads slowed the vehicles' progress considerably. Furthermore, the two bridges near Oleśnica had been destroyed by the fleeing Poles and the pioneers had to quickly put together a makeshift bridge with rubber dinghies.

At around 1300, the crossing was effected, and the SS units launched an attack northeast of Stolec, where the Poles had in the meantime well entrenched themselves. The enemy's dogged resistance forced Dietrich to also engage Wilhelm Trabandt's III./LSSAH on the left flank, in an attempt to overwhelm the Polish defensive positions. The fighting lasted several hours, and the advance was only able to resume late that night.

The Leibstandarte reported that they had annihilated an entire Polish battalion in the Stolec Forest, but the Warta River, the main objective, had not yet been reached. The next day, Sepp Dietrich sent the III./LSSAH forward, which advanced without encountering much resistance, reaching the Warta at 0930, near Burzenin: the wooden bridge was damaged and once again the engineers were called into action to get it back on its feet. There were no enemy units in the sector, but Polish artillery created problems, such as the wounding of SS-Hstuf. Scheide, the regiment's engineer, who had to be evacuated. The river crossing was completed around 1330 by III./LSSAH units and at 1700 by the II./LSSAH.

General Herbert Loch.

Beyond the river stretched a vast plain, under the control of Polish artillery well positioned about 7 kilometers away on the bank of the Widawka, a tributary of the Warta. The Gorki and Rembieszow bridges had been destroyed, and the SS units were stalled again. The day was marked by fresh losses in the unit. There was also criticism from General der Artillerie Herbert Loch, commander of the 17. Infanteriedivision, who complained of the poor use of the SS units in the field but above all of the fact that the villages where the shots had been fired had been systematically torched, thus depriving the troops of shelter for the night and creating further obstacles for the troops on the march.[2]

On September 5, Dietrich launched his units to attack the Widawka. But without adequate artillery support, since the II./Art.Rgt.46 had been temporarily transferred to support the 17 .Infanteriedivision, the

2 NARA, T-354/609. Divisionsbefehl für das Verhalten der Truppe im Operationsgebiet. 4.9.1939. In the order, Loch did not cite the Leibstandarte precisely, but the "motorized troops subordinate to him"—in practice, Dietrich's men.

SS-Ustuf. Otto Baum.

action ended in stalemate and the unit suffered three deaths and 33 wounded. In the evening, the order arrived to entrench in situ. In the meantime, other units of XIII. Armeekorps had managed to overwhelm the Polish positions along the Widawka.

During the night of September 5/6, the recon patrols reported that the enemy was fleeing, but on the morning of the 6th the order reached the Leibstandarte to fall back behind the Warta, on both sides of the Burzenin–Redzen road, where batteries from II./Art.Rgt.46 also duly arrived. The next day, the SS unit resumed its march, with the order to reach the Rzgow sector, still under the 17. Infanteriedivision.

Loch's division, reinforced by the tanks of I./Pz.Rgt.23, had been ordered to subdue the position at Lask and then continue toward Pabianice, which was to be defended until the arrival of the Leibstandarte. The objective was to isolate Lodz from the south by ensuring control of the dominant sector of Antoniew. The city of Pabianice was defended by a determined Polish group, which had been ordered to hold the position for as long as possible to allow the Poznan Army to extract itself from the pocket that had been created around it and at the same time cover the troops attempting to establish a defensive front on the road to Warsaw. Due to the destruction of the Grabia and Przygon bridges, the SS units were forced to carry out a vast bypass movement through the villages of Orpelow, Markowka, and Dobro, along sandy tracks, which significantly slowed the advance.

Kurt Meyer's testimony on this fighting:

> On September 7, around 1000, we reached the outskirts of Pabianice, with orders to establish blocking positions along the Rzgów–Wola–Ragowa–Lodz line. Pabianice was defended by strong enemy units with antitank weapons. The attack of the I./Pz.Rgt.23 was therefore repelled by the Polish defenders. Some destroyed German tanks lay immobilized. They had been out of action by the Polish antitank rifles. The Leibstandarte then took charge of the mission that was supposed to have been carried out by the tanks and immediately launched the attack. The 1. and 2. Kompanien managed to penetrate the town, opening the way for the rest of the battalion. Faced with the vigor of our attack, the Poles retreated to the town center, and immediately afterward determined enemy counterattacks were launched against the exposed flank of the regiment. The advanced firing positions of II./Art.Rgt.46 defended themselves desperately from the continuous attacks

> of the Polish infantry. There was fighting everywhere, the Polish units retreating from the west attacked, paying no heed to their heavy losses. Often, the regimental headquarters became the focal point of the fighting. Service personnel and drivers had to fight for their lives. The Poles advanced with difficulty toward the regimental staff, through a potato field and were visible for only a fraction of a second, as the foliage allowed them to hide well. We couldn't stop the enemy infantrymen from continuing to gain ground and getting almost within hand-grenade range. I jumped and started shooting into the potato field. It was the only chance to hit the Poles. On my right, there was a soldier from 13. Kompanie who was firing round after round as if he were practicing, on the attacking Poles. But our target practice didn't last long. Suddenly, I found myself at the bottom of the trench and I remember taking a bullet in my left shoulder. A bullet had pierced my shoulder and knocked me to the ground. My neighbor had fallen, a bullet through his neck. I was no longer capable of repelling another attack without support. From one side to the other, the fighting continued, and only after midday, the momentum of the attacking Poles was dampened.

Threatened with encirclement, the LSSAH 1. and 2. Kompanien were forced to retreat, so it was decided to resume the attack at 1530, bypassing Pabianice from the south and north, in the direction of Rzgow. The fresh attack began well and at 1630, I./LSSAH reported that it had reached the road north, between Pabianice and Konstantynow, while II./LSSAH had secured control of the road south of Pabianice to Huta. At the same time, however, II./Art. Rgt.46 was attacked by Polish cavalry units and farther south, Leibstandarte Adolf Hitler supply columns were also attacked. Soon after, Polish infantry units attacked II./LSSAH in the Kol.Bychlew sector. Otto Baum's 7. Kompanie lost four men during this fighting.

Sepp Dietrich, center, with Leibstandarte troops.

German soldiers in a Polish village, September 1939.

SS-Ustuf. Otto Baum's testimony criticizes Dietrich's command:

> The Poles emerged from the Czyzeminek Forest and from the west; shouting "Hurrah," they attacked my right flank which had been under their fire since the beginning. Based on my experience, which led me to the command of a division, I would never have launched this attack without first eliminating the enemy forces on the flanks.

II./LSSAH also complained of the loss and wounding of many officers, including SS-Hstuf. Mohnke, commander of the 5. Kompanie, and SS-Ostuf. Anhalt and Laesch, platoon commanders in the 7. and 8. Kompanien respectively. At 1700, SS-Ogruf. Dietrich ordered his units to maintain their positions and at the same time asked for assistance from the 10. Infanteriedivision, believing he was surrounded. Around 1830, enemy pressure began to decrease, just as the 5. Kompanie Infanterieregiment 55 arrived in the sector as reinforcements. In the evening, the situation definitively stabilized.

On September 8, the German advance continued north. The XIII. Armeekorps was to attack Lodz with the 10. Infanteriedivision from the north and northeast and with the 17. Infanteriedivision from the south and the west. At 0800, the Leibstandarte, still under the 17. Infanteriedivision, attacked Pabianice again, encountering little resistance and continuing in the direction of Rzgow. Once in position, Dietrich positioned his units to prevent any enemy counterattacks from the north, northeast, east, and southeast. But no further fighting occurred as the Poles had been routed. They had abandoned Lodz without a fight and had ended up in a large pocket west of Warsaw and the Vistula. The Polish capital was being threatened by General Erich Hoepner's XIV. Armeekorps and the 4. Panzerdivision reconnaissance group was already fighting on the southeastern outskirts of the city. The German command expected strong resistance from the remaining Polish forces retreating from the Western Front toward Warsaw and therefore decided to transfer the Leibstandarte to the XIV. Armeekorps and specifically to Generalleutnant Georg-Hans Reinhardt's 4. Panzerdivision engaged on two fronts west of the Polish capital.

On September 9, early in the morning, the SS units set out for the Falenty–Nadarzyn sector, where they arrived at around 1800, greeted by General Hoepner himself, who welcomed the new reinforcements, as can be seen from the report made by the commander of 4. Panzerdivision himself:

> The morning attack against the city was interrupted due to numerous losses. Warsaw is defended by well-armed and well-entrenched enemy troops in solid and extensive fortifications, which one single armored division with four infantry battalions cannot overcome. Since the occupation of the city is of minor significance on a military level, I propose to suspend the attacks and that the 4. Panzerdivision, leaving some troops to cover in the direction of Warsaw, moves to new positions along the roads used by the Polish forces retreating from the west toward the capital. For this mission, the 4. Panzerdivision, which is fighting alone in the enemy's rear, would need additional infantry support since the Panzers cannot serve as a covering force.

General Hoepner approved Reinhardt's analysis and ordered the transfer of the 4. Panzerdivision. It was necessary to reinforce his left flank, defended only by the reconnaissance battalion Aufklärungs-Abteilung 7 and an artillery battery. The Leibstandarte was chosen as reinforcements: the order was to take a position north of the Bzura River to prevent the Polish troops, pushed back toward the southeast by Army Group North, from crossing the river and joining the Warsaw garrison. At the same time, the Eighth and Tenth Armies were to surround the Polish forces in a triangle located west of Kutno, where the Bzura flows into the Vistula, near Wyszogrod.

On the night of September 9/10, the Leibstandarte therefore began to deploy north and the LSSAH motorcycle company, the 15.(Kradsch.)Kp., was immediately sent to Nowa Wies to reinforce Aufkl.Abt.7, which from that moment was placed under the control of the SS regiment. The SS motorcyclists were to take up positions around the villages of Domaniew and Moszna, on both banks of the Utrata River. They were followed by the II./LSSAH which

General Erich Hoepner.

Generalleutnant Reinhardt.

German Panzers advance into Polish territory, September 1939.

German motorized column on the march.

Members of the Obrona Narodowa Polish militia in an ambush position.

was to defend the Oltarzew sector and by the I./LSSAH which was to deal with the Domaniew sector. Artillery support would be provided by II./Art.Rgt.103. However, when the SS units arrived in the area, numerous Polish columns had penetrated the villages of Oltarzew and Ozarow. Undaunted, Kohlroser's soldiers engaged in battle and destroyed the enemy forces. The other Polish columns, sensing the danger, attempted to pass farther north, so the III./LSSAH was deployed to Macierzysz, blocking them. The I. and II./LSSAH reported capturing at least 1,200 Polish troops during the night. The Poles had suffered terrible losses, but some units had nevertheless managed to continue to Warsaw during the night.

German soldiers during an attack.

On September 10, the 4. Panzerdivision then ordered the Leibstandarte to establish a link with the 31. Infanteriedivision west of Pruszkow. 1. Panzerdivision had meanwhile established a bridgehead on the Vistula near

A mortar supports an infantry assault.

Otwok, so the 4. Panzerdivision was ordered to extend its blocking line: the Leibstandarte was ordered to establish new defensive positions along the Pilaszkow–Josefow railway line, between the Utrata and the Rokitnica Rivers to prevent Polish troops from reaching Warsaw from the Blonie area. The I./LSSAH positioned itself on the right and the II./LSSAH on the left. Each battalion was reinforced by a platoon of infantry support guns and a platoon of antitank guns. On the right flank everything went smoothly, while on the left, von Oberkamp's men encountered strong resistance in Plochocin, Kopytow, and Swiecice. The assigned objectives were reached at 1800 and a new defensive line was established between Pilaszkow, Lazniew, and Jozefow, which was immediately attacked by the Poles, but without success.

During the night, the III./LSSAH extended the regiment's right wing northward. Fighting continued during the morning of September 11 and then decreased in intensity around midday. The next day the SS units found themselves in a pincer movement, having to face enemy attacks coming from the sector north of Sochaczew and from the Leszno–Kampinow sector.

From the report of 6. Kompanie LSSAH:

> The 6. Kompanie had its first day of rest on September 11. We moved into a very large village called Swiecice around noon. Around 10 p.m., the sentry on duty in front of the company command post reported antitank gunfire coming from the east at varying distances along the road and on both sides of it. His report, however, was not taken into consideration, as the sentry was considered unreliable. However, the shooting continued to intensify, so the company commander was awakened. He then went to the road and confirmed the report. The company was immediately put on alert and took up positions along a road that started from the main road and headed south. When the first elements of the company arrived, the enemy was already a hundred meters away. We threw ourselves into the ditch,

German motorized units in Poland, September 1939.

with our rifles and machine guns ready to open fire. The first enemy elements quickly attacked, shouting. We immediately returned their fire. Bullets whistled on all sides, some grenades exploded behind us, and a Polish machine gun started firing at our side. Our company commander, SS-Hstuf. Rudolf Lange, ordered us to cease fire. We had to change our position.

A Pz.Kpfw. I Ausf B advances.

Attack on a Polish village with fire support from an antitank gun and an armored car, September 1939.

While retreating northward, 6. Kompanie encountered the I./LSSAH units that had been sent to attack the positions of Pilaszkow and Witki, which were overwhelmed thanks to the fire support from 4. Batterie Artillerieregiment 103. LSSAH's 3. Kompanie was then sent to Swiecice, to regain the lost sector. After contacting the enemy, violent fighting broke out. 3. Kompanie being outnumbered, the battalion's reserve platoons arrived as reinforcements, while the remnants of 6. Kompanie were engaged under the command of SS-Ustuf. Kaschula, orderly officer of I./LSSAH. The Poles were eventually repelled, thanks above all to the direct fire of 4. Batterie. Kurt Meyer's testimony on these last battles follows:

Polish cavalry units on the move.

Leibstandarte soldiers engaged in a firefight.

During the night of September 12/13 a strong enemy unit had managed to penetrate the positions of the II./LSSAH; the opening of a large breach seemed imminent. In the early hours of the morning the news reached us that the 6. Kompanie had been overwhelmed, and its commander had fallen in combat. I was particularly attached to him. Since 1929 we had been part of the same large unit. The report on the enemy penetration that threatened us seemed incredible. We couldn't believe that the enemy had managed to break our positions. I was ordered to verify the accuracy of the information. I jumped into the saddle of a sidecar and disappeared in the direction of Blonie.

German troops cross a river on a wooden bridge built by pioneers.

German soldiers and a village on fire.

German units engaged in the Pabianice sector, September 1939.

A Pz.Kpfw. III moving into the attack, September 1939.

Leibstandarte soldiers engaged in the Pabianice area. Note that the soldiers have covered their wristbands, to hide the name of their unit from the enemy.

A Pz.Kpfw. I crosses a stream in Poland.

A Polish Bofors wz.36 3.7-cm antitank piece.

An MG 34 in defensive position, September 1939.

German motorcycle riflemen engaged in attacking Polish units hidden in a forest.

A Pz.Kpfw. II engaged in a Polish village.

SS-Obersturmführer Pfeiffer, who would die heroically a few years later as commander of a Panther company, also went up and accompanied me. At great speed we traveled along the "death road" quickly to avoid the insects and the pestilential stench that rose from the carcasses of the dead animals along it. A few hundred meters in front of Swiecice, I saw two Polish soldiers and a soldier from the 6. Kompanie behind a small bridge. The behavior of the three soldiers seemed strange, so I braked sharply, jumped from the motorcycle and headed toward the group kneeling in a ditch. When I reached the edge of it, I understood the reason for their strange behavior. The soldier was a prisoner of the Poles and looked at me with a dismayed expression when he saw me advancing alone toward the group. Damnation! I had once again gotten lucky! Pfeiffer's machine gun had prevented the Poles from sending me to the other world. It was therefore true: the 6. Kompanie had been overwhelmed, and its commander was lying in the ditch a

Polish cavalry units, September 1939.

Polish cavalry launched into the attack.

few hundred meters in front of us. Pfeiffer and I continued to approach Swiecice and found our fallen comrade. A bullet to the chest had ended his life. Seppel Lange was dead, an exemplary soldier. We will never forget it.

An MG 34 of the Leibstandarte in Poland.

Two Pz.Kpfw. Is on a Polish road, September 1939.

Pz.Kpfw. IV tanks in a Polish town on the eve of an action, September 1939.

Polish infantry in combat, September 1939.

The former positions of II./LSSAH were retaken at about 1100. The enemy breakthrough was blocked by I./LSSAH from the north and II./LSSAH from the west, thanks also to the support of II./Pz.Rgt.36 and II./Inf.Rgt.33. Immediately after midday, the Polish units returned to attack again, particularly in the I./LSSAH sector at Zaborow and Pilaszkow. The SS battalion managed to push them back thanks to the intervention of I./Pz.Rgt.36, and then withdrew in the late afternoon in the direction of Konotopa.

A Pz.Kpfw. II in combat.

Rudolf Lange was born January 31, 1910, in Tiebensee, SS-Nr. 51 421. He was killed on September 12, 1939, at Swiecice.

Herbert Kaschula was born on September 23, 1912, in Lichterfelde, Berlin, SS-Nr. 23 708. He had served previously in 3./LSSAH.

Hans Pfeiffer was born on December 5, 1915 in Hamberge, Schleswig-Holstein, SS-Nr. 173 987. He had served previously in I./Sta. Germania in 1935 before being transferred to LSSAH's Panzer-Späh-zug (Panzer scout train) in 1938. He would later command 6. SS-Panzerregiment 12 but would die in Normandy on June 12, 1944, as commander of 4. SS-Panzerregiment 12.

Artur Klingemeier was born February 24, 1913, at Kummerfeld, SS-Nr. 25 936.

Fritz Beutler was born April 28, 1910, in Berlin, SS-Nr. 34 783. He had served previously in 1. Kompanie LSSAH.

On the Bzura Front

The concentration of numerous Polish forces in the Bzura River sector forced the German headquarters to review its plans: on September 13, XIV. Armeekorps was therefore transferred west of the river in the direction of Sochaczew and Kutno, being temporarily subordinated to the Eighth Army. The German plan aimed at the annihilation of the Polish forces between the Bzura and the Vistula, with a concentric offensive of the Eighth and Tenth Armies, supported from above by Luftflotte 4 (Air Fleet 4). XIV. Armeekorps was to block the exit of enemy forces from the Bzura pocket from the east, attacking from Sochaczew in the direction of the Vistula. On September 13, the corps launched the attack with 4. Panzerdivision and 31. Infanteriedivision, having as their first objective that of surrounding the Polish troops east of Blonie. Initially the Leibstandarte was ordered to sweep the sector between Lezno, Pialuty, and Wasy in the evening. SS-Ogruf. Dietrich took advantage of this

German Panzers cross the Bzura River, September 1939.

A Polish armored railway train carrying tanks, captured by the Leibstandarte in the Blonie area, September 1939.

relatively calm day to reorganize his units and appoint SS-Hstuf. Klingemeier to command 6. Kompanie and SS-Ostuf. Beutler as liaison officer to II./LSSAH.

The next day, the Leibstandarte was again attached to 4. Panzerdivision, which was to continue its attack westward to block the sector from Sochaczew to the Vistula and prevent the Polish troops from making for the capital. The SS units were assigned to the Kampfgruppe Hartlieb, consisting of elements of Panzerbrigade 5. and began deploying around 0900. The I./LSSAH attacked Sochaczew with the support of an armored battalion from Panzerregiment 36 and an artillery group from Artillerieregiment Kempny. Violent

A Polish road congested by the passage of German motorized columns, September 1939.

German tanks and motorcycle scouts on the outskirts of a Polish village, September 1939.

fighting immediately broke out in the streets and houses of the town—the position changed hands three times during the day.

Around 2000, 4. Panzerdivision reported that the Brochow–Sochaczew sector had been captured, but the two positions were lost again during the night, due to a massive bombardment by Polish artillery. From the testimonies of some prisoners, it emerged that the Poles were massing numerous forces west of the Bzura to attempt to push in the direction of Warsaw. During the night, small groups of soldiers attempted to reach the Polish capital, alerting not only the SS units but also those of 4. Panzerdivision. On September 15, the Leibstandarte was engaged in repelling some localized enemy attacks, which resulted in only a few injuries.

An MG 34 in firing position, Poland, September 1939.

German artillery in action on the Polish front.

Around midday, the XVI. Armeekorps once again passed under the control of von Reichenau's Tenth Army. The new orders for 4. Panzerdivision and the Leibstandarte, established for the following day, were the crossing of the Bzura and the capture of the road located two kilometers west of that river. On September 16, at 0700, the II., I., and III./LSSAH crossed the river one after the other, using a footbridge built by the SS engineers, near Plecewice. II./Pz.Rgt.35 also crossed the river to support the SS units. The advance stopped in front of the village of Bibijampol, where a strong counterattack by the Poles put the German units in some difficulty. The situation was reestablished thanks to German artillery fire, which destroyed the enemy units.

An Sd.Kfz. 6 halftrack towing a 10.5-cm FeldHaubitze 18 leichte, advancing on the Bzura front, followed by a Horch command vehicle, September 1939.

German tanks and motorcyclists in Poland.

Around midday, the I./LSSAH took the village of Juliopol, while II./LSSAH managed to push as far as D.Ruski. The attack did not continue further, as groups of Polish soldiers had barricaded themselves in several farms and in the woods, continuing to resist. Furthermore, II./LSSAH failed to dislodge the Polish defenders entrenched inside the village of Adamowa Gora. The tenacious resistance and several counterattacks by the enemy convinced Generalleutnant Reinhardt to order the withdrawal of the most advanced units threatened with being cut off. A new defensive line was established between Gawlow Lubianka in the south and Helenka, Bibijampol, and Juljupol in the northwest. At 1900, II./LSSAH relieved I./LSSAH, which was placed in reserve at Zukowka, while the 15.(Kradsch.)Kp./LSSAH was employed to cover the right flank north of Plecewice.

On September 17, a Polish battalion attacked in this last sector, forcing the Leibstandarte to deploy all its reserves, including the regimental staff, to repel the enemy. The Polish battalion was annihilated, having sacrificed itself in some suicidal charges. In the early afternoon, the Leibstandarte headquarters was attacked by Polish aircraft, but no losses

A German 3.7-cm antitank piece.

Motorized units of the Leibstandarte on the march.

were recorded. A few minutes later, 1. Kompanie LSSAH reported that it had captured a staff car carrying a Polish general and three general staff officers. The general was the commander of the 17th Infantry Division and from the documents found in his possession, the enemy's offensive for the following day was revealed. The German headquarters then learned that they had been attacked by the 14th and 25th Infantry Divisions, reinforced by the Polish 17th Division, which had been ordered to cross the Bzura River.

However, the attack on September 16 by 4. Panzerdivision and the Leibstandarte had ruined the Polish plans. Generalleutnant Reinhardt then decided to attack east of the river northward with all available forces. To cover the attack of Panzerregiment 36 on Brochow, III./LSSAH deployed to the western bank of the Bzura, near Mistrzewice, receiving support from a company of the same Panzerregiment 36: during the transfer march the SS units engaged in a short but violent fight with enemy units, destroying them.

Also on September 17, Soviet forces entered Poland from the east and four days later, they reached the demarcation line established in the Molotov–Ribbentrop Pact. On September 18, the Leibstandarte was relieved from the western bank of the Bzura by elements of the 19. Infanteriedivision and 1. Panzerdivision. Except for I./LSSAH, all other units were to be grouped between Pasikonie, Kaskie, Knatovice, and Zawady. I./LSSAH was instead assigned to the Kampfgruppe Hartlieb, with the task of supporting II./Pz.Rgt.36 in its attack in the direction of Sladow, a town located south of the Vistula. At approximately 1000, the Panzers crossed the Lasica River and the Sladow position was captured at 1300.

The Polish troops in the sector were now surrounded. But they did not lose heart, counterattacking ferociously and in turn managing to surround I./LSSAH which found itself fighting with its back to the Vistula, while II./Pz.Rgt.36, heavily engaged in Sladow, attacked from the east. Other units of 4. Panzerdivision were attacked near Prszeslawicew and in Gorki, remaining surrounded. Generalleutnant Reinhardt's command post in Tutowice found itself under enemy attack. The Leibstandarte was called to their aid and set out during the night, arriving in position at dawn on September 19, placing itself at Reinhardt's disposal.

SS-Ogruf. Sepp Dietrich.

The I./LSSAH was still surrounded east of Sladow and was starting to run low on ammunition.

Thanks to a breakthrough by some tanks from Panzerregiment 36, it was possible to resupply the SS units, allowing them to continue to resist. Meanwhile, Generalleutnant Reinhardt organized his counterattack to free the encircled units, having only Pz.Rgt.35, Schtz.Rgt.12, I./Schtz. Rgt.33, and the Leibstandarte at his disposal. The orders were then issued: Pz.Rgt.35 forward, supported by III./ LSSAH, while II./LSSAH was to cover their left flank. Schtz.Rgt.12 and I./ Schtz.Rgt.33 were to follow II./LSSAH and then push toward the Bzura southeast of Preslawice. The artillery would cover the advance by hitting the Bzura valley. The attack was launched at 0800 and an hour later, Panzerregiment 35 had already managed to link up with Panzerregiment 36. The Leibstandarte units advanced more slowly, having to destroy nests of enemy resistance along the road. I./LSSAH was relieved at around 1100.

Polish defensive position on the Bzura front, 1939.

Following is the testimony of Hubert Meyer, platoon commander of 10. Kompanie LSSAH, on the fighting that day:

> We had attacked in the morning with light tanks and were grouped near a railway embankment. Right in front of us, there was a hill covered by small trees, behind which we thought the enemy was. When we were about 600 meters from it, violent machine-gun fire forced us to take cover. The panzers stopped to look for their targets. I ran toward the nearest panzer, hit the turret with the butt of my gun and reported the position of an enemy machine-gun nest to the tank commander. He opened fire while I was still close to the tank. The sound of the shooting almost made me deaf for the rest of the day. The tanks then began to advance rapidly again. We followed them slowly. When they were 100 meters from the hill, the Poles waved white flags. The panzers then continued to advance.
>
> When we reached the same distance, the flags disappeared, and we came under enemy fire again. If we had remained in that position, we would have been killed one after the other. I then gave the order to attack the hill. The Poles fled after a violent hand-to-hand battle. We did not suffer any losses. It was now necessary to reach the panzers as soon as possible. Behind the hill was a strip of meadow about 200 meters wide and then a forest. Slightly to the right we spotted a stopped panzer; around the vehicle, there were Poles trying to open the doors. We immediately started shooting at them. I had a Polish carbine with me. Surprised, the Poles returned fire but became furious when they saw several of my men running in the direction of the panzer. Neither we nor the Poles won that battle, but the panzer was liberated. Its crew thanked us and were grateful. Another panzer had ended up in a ditch full of water, but no noise came from inside. I put

Leibstandarte soldiers on the streets of Sochaczew.

Leibstandarte troops engaged in a firefight in the streets of Sochaczew.

my platoon back in formation and we continued toward the Vistula. When we emerged from the forest, we found ourselves facing fields full of fruit trees that extended toward a road about 700 meters away; the road passed through the fields in the direction of the attack. The Poles we had put to flight were digging in. Our panzers had disappeared from our sight.

But we couldn't give the enemy time to recover and therefore we had to continue without armored support. We were forced to continue the march knowing that the enemy would make us advance and then hit us at an optimal distance. If I had sent a patrol forward, it would surely have been suicide. But who could help us? We only had to rely on ourselves. All I had to do was put myself at the head of the platoon advance in attack formation. I had to use all my courage to do this. The closer we got to the road, the more the tension increased. We looked so intently around us that we felt as if our eyes were about to pop out of their sockets, but we saw nothing. We were 100 meters from the road. The first pitch would come, and it would surely be meant for me. At that distance they couldn't miss me. I was very tense; my heart was pounding. I was waiting for the first shot. My legs kept moving forward. But no enemy shots. We reached some houses. There was no one to be seen. Just some pigs in the yard of the next house. The tension slowly eased. We looked at each other, almost embarrassed. Everyone knew that the others had experienced the same tension. We then crossed the meadows to reach the Vistula and fired a flare. It was at that point that violent gunfire erupted.

Bullets began to whiz through the air, branches fell to the ground. But there was no enemy to be seen. One of our panzers arrived, but it couldn't fire. Then an armored car appeared. I went up on it to talk to its commander and then I saw some Polish helmets on the left behind an embankment near the river. So that was where the enemy was shooting from. After having my mortar adjusted and then

> fired at a high rate, I advanced with my men on the left to attempt to reach the embankment. I couldn't see if my men were following me, but I knew very well that they would never leave me alone. The Poles had taken cover in their individual foxholes to avoid mortar fire. A close combat ensued. Fortunately, I had the Polish carbine with me. While I was engaging in hand-to-hand combat with a Polish soldier, another emerged from a ditch along the river; I did not see him. But, my courier, SS-Sturmmann Spiekhofen, who was following me closely, killed him. We took more than 60 prisoners, including a colonel. We were completely exhausted, physically and emotionally. All the men lay down on the ground and fell asleep on the spot. A noncommissioned officer told me about Spiekhofen's intervention. I shook his hand. What else could I have done? Life is everything but it is always hanging by a thread. You can lose it at any moment, as if nothing had happened.

The fighting that day was particularly bloody and was characterized by violent episodes, such as the cold-blooded killing of some German soldiers: SS-Ostuf. Brüchmann, platoon leader in 14. Kompanie LSSAH and an SS noncommissioned officer, after being wounded, were captured by Polish soldiers. Shortly afterward, they were found dead, horribly mutilated.

At around 1100, Generalleutnant Reinhardt was able to announce that all encircled German units had been liberated. The battle of the Bzura had ended with a complete victory and the destruction of two Polish armies, the capture of 105,000 prisoners, of which 20,000 were claimed by 4. Panzerdivision and the Leibstandarte. Polish forces were now resisting only in Warsaw and at the fortified area of Modlin, about 20 kilometers northwest of the capital. The Leibstandarte, except for its II./LSSAH, was taken over for transfer to the Fw.Paski–Zawady–Gnatowice sector, for a short rest. The II./LSSAH remained in the theater to destroy the last pockets of enemy resistance.

Units of the Leibstandarte following an armored car enter Sochaczew.

Leibstandarte troops during the fighting inside Sochaczew.

A Leibstandarte Sd.Kfz. 232 engaged in Poland.

Stukas and a Panzer in Poland, September 1939.

Johannes Brüchmann was born on August 24, 1911, at Erfde in Holstein, SS-Nr. 10 367. Wounded and captured, he was executed and his body was mutilated by his Polish captors.

Fights in the Modlin Area

On September 21, after a day of rest, during which the men were mainly busy cleaning their weapons and vehicles, the Leibstandarte was transferred to XV. Armeekorps of General der Infanterie Hermann Hoth. The corps had been ordered to attack the Modlin Fortress from the south, while from the north II. Armeekorps would attack. At 0700, SS-Ogruf. Dietrich received orders to move his unit to the Kol.Lubiec–Wiersce sector. The advance of the SS units was significantly hampered by the poor state of the roads, which forced the men to get out of their vehicles and march on foot. Once they arrived at the new sector, the Leibstandarte was attached to the 29. Infanteriedivision of Generalleutnant Joachim Lemelsen, except for I./LSSAH, which remained at the disposal of XV. Armeekorps in the area between Leszno and Kol.Lubiec. The next day, the bulk of the regiment moved into the Wiersce area, except for II./LSSAH, which was busy clearing the wooded region of Janowec.

In the evening, the Leibstandarte received orders to relieve several army battalions holding the Dobrozyn–Malocice–Czeczothki sector, moving the battle line forward about 300 meters. Artillery support would be provided by I./Art.Rgt.65. At dawn on September 23, the operation began: I./LSSAH took position on the left flank and III./LSSAH on the

German Panzers cross a watercourse in Poland thanks to a bridge built by pioneers.

German motorcycle scouts in a Polish village.

Leibstandarte soldiers waiting on the side of a Polish road, during a transfer march.

Leibstandarte troops drive through a destroyed Polish village.

right, while II./LSSAH remained behind to ensure the protection of the ammunition east of Janowec and to maintain connection with Infanterieregiment 71. Polish artillery immediately began to pound the SS companies on the front line. Some captured Polish prisoners reported that the troops defending the Modlin stronghold were about to attempt a sortie toward the capital during the night. At dusk, II./LSSAH was also transferred to the front line, taking over I./Inf.Rgt.15. On its left were 2. leichte-Division echelons. Fort "V" was in front of the positions defended by Leibstandarte units. On September 24, no significant clashes occurred, apart from some artillery fire. At dawn the next day, some Polish deserters reported that inside the fortress ammunition and food supplies had begun to run out and the morale of the troops had dropped significantly. During the morning, commander Sepp Dietrich followed the

An SS-Sturmmann of the Leibstandarte.

Polish prisoners, September 1939.

15.(Kradsch.)Kp./LSSAH to Guzow, to welcome the Führer and accompany him on his inspection of the front. The next day, I./LSSAH was taken over by a battalion from 221. Infanteriedivision and transferred to the reserve south of Brzozowka.

In the afternoon, two patrols formed with elements of II. and III./LSSAH were sent toward Fort "V" to evaluate whether the Poles were actually ready to surrender. But they were met with gunfire and two soldiers were killed. During the night of September 27/28, the Leibstandarte was relieved by Infanterieregiment 354 of 213. Infanteriedivision and transferred as a reserve for the Tenth Army in the Sochaczew–Bielice–Paprotnia sector. On September 29, with the last German assault on the fortress, the Poles capitulated.

On October 1, Sepp Dietrich received the order to transfer his unit to Prague, together with the SS-Pionier-Bataillon of the SS-Verfügungstruppe. The Leibstandarte was to replace the SS-Der Führer Regiment, which was transferred along the Westwall. And so ended the Polish campaign for the men of Leibstandarte Adolf Hitler, during which the Führer's bodyguard suffered the loss of 108 killed (including 8 officers), 292 wounded, and 4 missing.

A Leibstandarte defensive position south of Modlin, September 1939.

The Leibstandarte during a transfer march on the Modlin front.

Polish General Wiktor Thommée, commander of the Modlin Fortress, negotiates surrender with German General Adolf Strauß, September 29, 1939.

Leibstandarte troops on parade, 1939.

Panzerdivision Kempf in Action

On September 1, at 0445, military operations against Poland began. Forces of Küchler's Third Army, including the Panzerverband—Panzerdivision Kempf—crossed the border, penetrating northern Mazovia. Panzerdivision Kempf advanced on the right flank of 1. Kavallerie-Brigade. General Kempf ordered the SS-Aufklärungs-Abteilung to send reconnaissance patrols toward Bialuty and the forests farther west, while other German forces began attacking the Mlawa position, defended by the Polish 20th Infantry Division.

However, initial attacks launched by the 61. Infanteriedivision were repelled. The intervention of SS-Standartenführer Felix Steiner's Deutschland Regiment was requested. Steiner was ordered to open a breach in the enemy defenses, attacking in the direction of the city of Mlawa,

Adolf Hitler reviews Leibstandarte troops in Poland, September 1939.

In Profile:
Felix Steiner (1896–1966)

Steiner was born on May 23, 1896, in Stalluponen, East Prussia. He joined the Royal Prussian Army as an infantry cadet. During World War I, he was awarded the Iron Cross 1st and 2nd Class. In 1919, he joined the Freikorps in the East Prussian city of Memel during the German Revolution and was later incorporated into the Reichswehr in 1921. In 1933, he left the army as a major. He then joined the Nazi Party and the SA. In 1935 he joined the SS and enlisted in the SS-VT. In 1936 he was promoted to *SS-Standartenführer* and took command of the SS-Deutschland Regiment. He took part in the invasion of Poland and the battle for France, being awarded the Knight's Cross of the Iron Cross on August 15, 1940. He was then instructed by Himmler to create and command the SS-Division Viking, which saw service on the Eastern Front. The division was particularly brutal, for example massacring 600 Jews in Zboriv, Ukraine. In April 1943, he took command of III. SS-Panzerkorps, which after seeing service in Yugoslavia, was transferred to the northern sector of the Eastern Front at Leningrad. His unit withdrew with Army Group North to the Courland (Kurland) Peninsula, whence the unit escaped to Germany to participate in the battle of Seelow Heights and the battle of Berlin, among others. He was imprisoned after the war until 1948 when he faced charges at Nuremberg, but the charges were dropped, and he was released. He was a founding member, in 1953, of HIAG, the denialist Waffen-SS lobby group. His memoirs, *Die Freiwilligen der Waffen-SS: Idee und Opfergang* (The Volunteers of Waffen-SS: Idea and Sacrifice), were published in 1958.

SS Gruppenführer und Generalleutnant der Waffen-SS Felix Steiner. (Bundesarchiv, Bild 146-1973-138-14A / CC-BY-SA 3.0)

Another photo of Hitler's visit to the Leibstandarte.

on both sides of the Napierken–Mlawa road. The Deutschland attack would be supported by divisional artillery fire. Steiner committed two battalions, the III. Deutschland on the right which was to capture the village of Dvierznis and the II. Deutschland on the left, which was to attack the village of Zavadski. The II. Deutschland remained under regimental control. Once the two positions had been occupied, the two battalions were then to proceed south, in the direction of Mlawa. The Deutschland units advanced without encountering any resistance until they reached Hill 192, where the Poles were solidly entrenched. As soon as the SS soldiers approached the position, they came under fire from the Poles' heavy weapons. Steiner sent scouting patrols out to find weak points in the enemy's defensive line.

What follows is the testimony of soldier Georg Prell, of the 3. Kompanie Deutschland, which provides an understanding of how the fighting in Zavadski took place:

Soldiers of the Deutschland Regiment training with a mortar, summer 1939.

SS-VT units prepare to attack Polish positions.

Polish defensive positions at Mlawa.

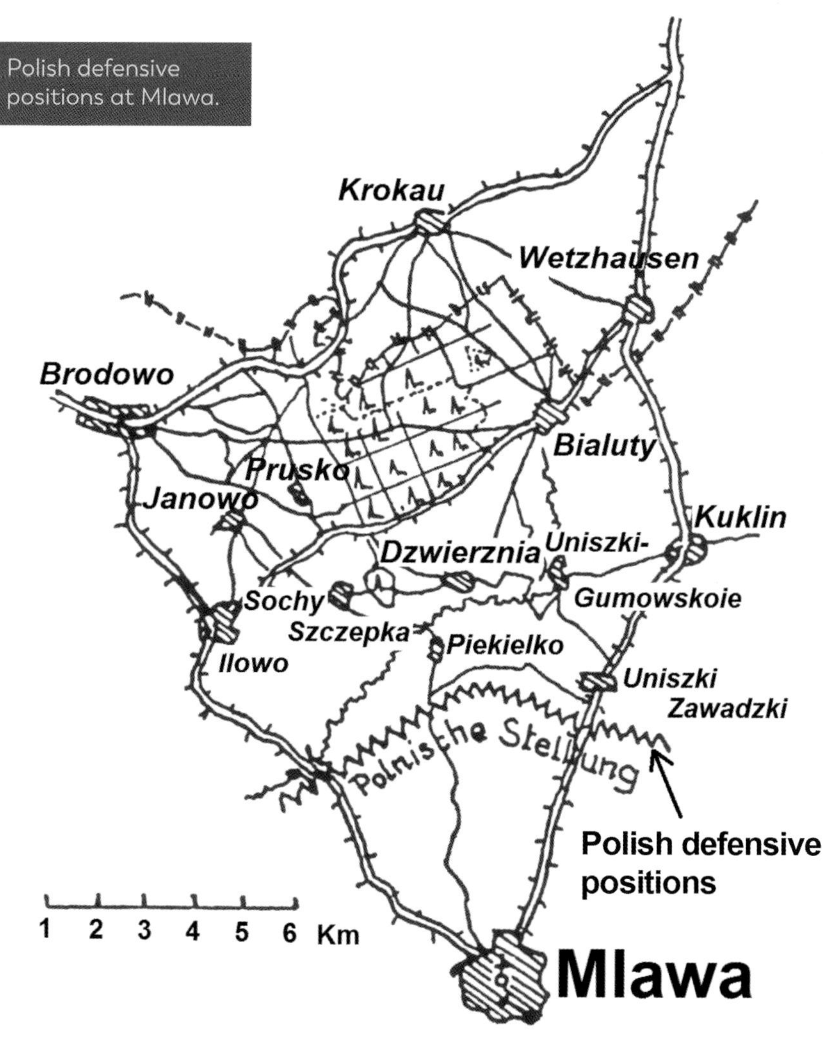

German tanks attacking Polish defensive positions, September 1939.

We had been at war for about six hours. Our company reached the village of Zavadski along our route of march. The Poles had extended barbed-wire barricades to protect them, behind which stood the hill from which the entire surrounding area was dominated. We couldn't stop, we had to be faster than the

Attack by a tank of Panzerregiment 7 followed by Deutschland infantry against the positions at Mlawa.

Deutschland infantry stalled by enemy fire.

A column of Deutschland marching on a Polish road, September 1939. (Carlo Fattoretto Collection)

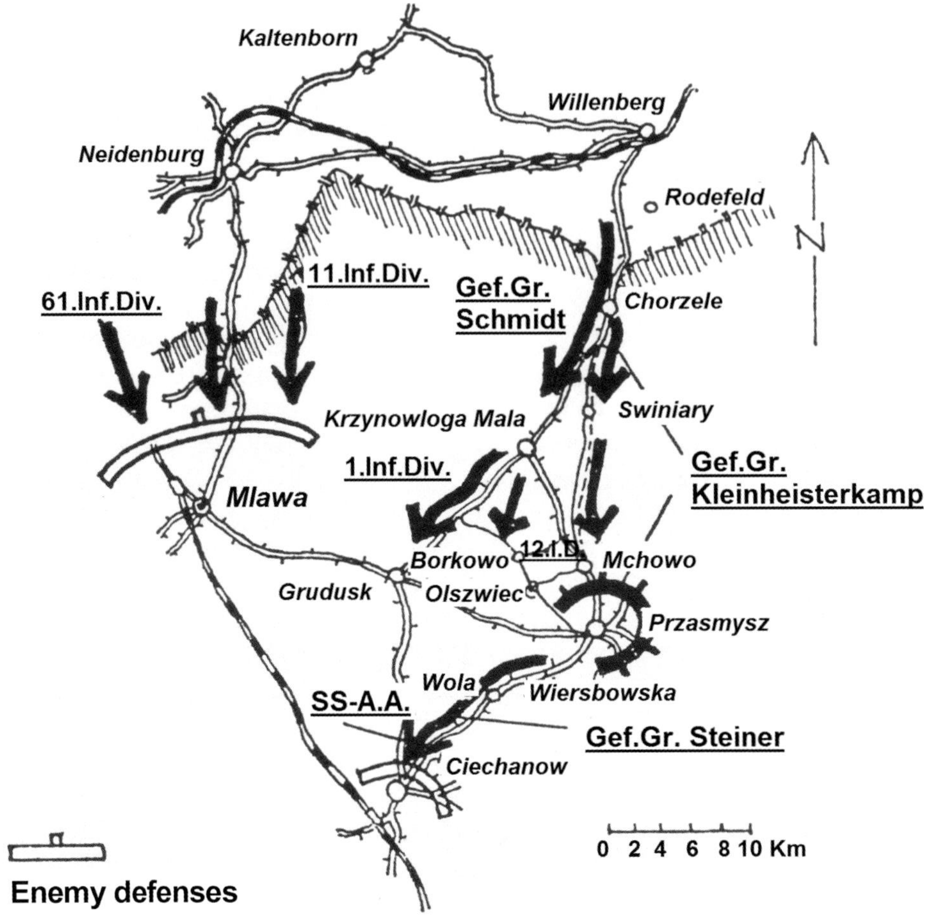

Movements of units between September 1 and 4, 1939.

> enemy. Unterscharführer Krieger with his platoon passed through the barbed wire attacking the Polish positions on the hill. The Poles responded with a massive barrage blocking our attack. Krieger was one of the first to be fatally hit by enemy fire and was also the first casualty of our company killed in combat. To overcome the enemy, we bypassed the heavily defended position and attacked in another sector, where we managed to open a passage.

At the same time, new orders and the promise of possible armored support arrived from the Heer headquarters.

The Deutschland was to continue to attack the hill frontally, engaging two assault groups along the flanks. The attack would be supported by the artillery and armored vehicles of Panzerregiment 7. The SS troops then attacked in the early afternoon, only to find themselves once again stalled by the enemy's massive barrage. Panzer support proved ineffective since the Poles had prepared solid antitank defenses, using sections of railway tracks driven into the concrete along the road, which blocked the tanks.

The few tanks that managed to overcome the obstacles ended up under fire from the Polish field artillery, forcing Oberst Landgraf to call off the attack and withdraw: seven tanks were destroyed and another 32 damaged. In this way, the SS soldiers were alone under the intense fire of Polish artillery and snipers. An assault group from I./Deutschland managed

SS-Staf. Felix Steiner (right) in Poland, 1939.

to get within a few meters of the first line of bunkers, before it too was stopped by enemy fire. Under the cover of darkness, all the German units withdrew in good order, returning to a safe distance from the Polish firing positions.

On September 2, the Panzerverband was moved to the Rodefeld sector, farther east, to attempt to outflank Mlawa. On this occasion, it was attached to General der Artillerie Albert Wodrig's Korps z.b.V. Wodrig and organized into three tactical groups: the battle group Gefechtsgruppe Steiner (including the bulk of the SS-Deutschland Regiment), the Gefechtsgruppe Kleinheisterkamp (III./Deutschland), and the Gefechtsgruppe Schmidt (Panzerregiment 7).

On September 3, the Panzerverband went over to the attack, advancing through Chorzele, Swiniary, Przasnysz, Wola, and Ciechanow, bypassing the Polish positions. Now isolated, the enemy units defending the Mlawa sector were forced to fall back. Following this success the Panzerverband was attached to III. Armeekorps, with the mission of crossing the Narew River at Rozan. The Deutschland assault groups together with Panzerregiment 7 harried the retreating Polish units up to Rozan, where the Poles set up a new defensive line structured around a series of bunkers dating back to the time of the Russian tsars.

A soldier of the Deutschland Regiment inspects the remains of a destroyed Polish convoy.

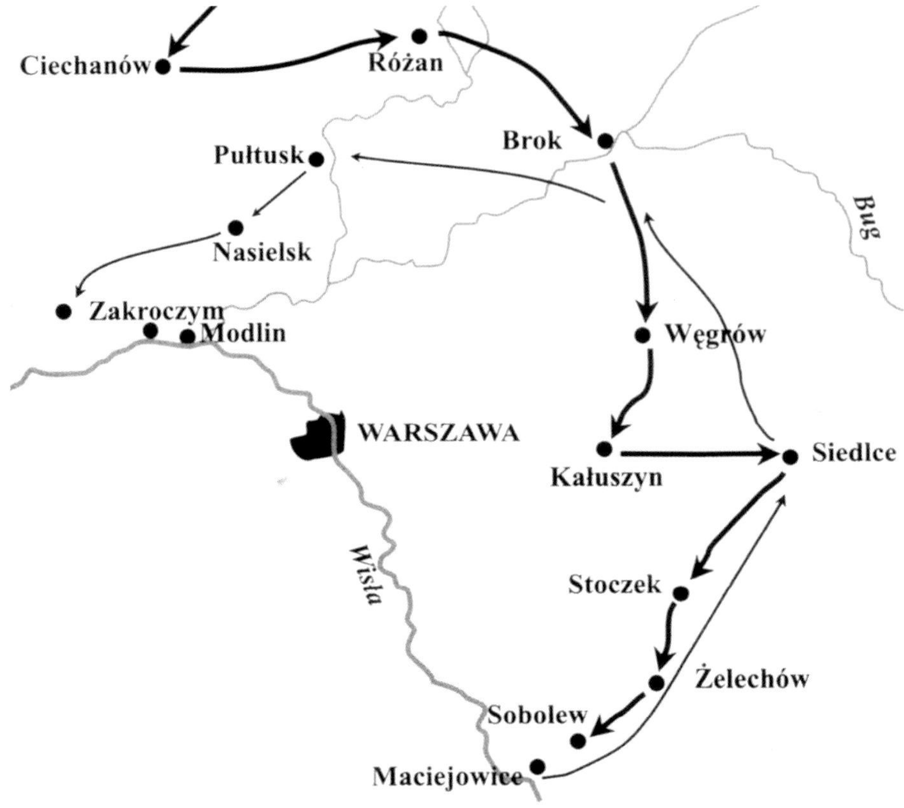

Movements of Panzerdivision Kempf between Ciechanow and Modlin.

The clashes that followed were terrible. Here too the SS units encountered bitter resistance from the Poles who, after repelling the initial German assaults, launched a series of ferocious counterattacks involving cavalry squadrons and light tank formations. During these battles, II./Pz.Rgt.7 lost another 11 tanks. However, overwhelming German firepower eventually forced the Polish garrison to lay down their arms. On September 8, the Panzerverband was subordinated to XXI. Armeekorps: this time the objective was the conquest of Lomza. Moving from Rozan, Gefechtsgruppe Steiner captured Czerwin and Nordbory. Meanwhile, the rest of the Panzerverband in turn captured the Ostrow-Mazowieka position. After this fresh success, Kempf's units, as of September 12, struck out to the southeast. The Panzerverband crossed the Bug River at Brok and engaged Polish forces at Kliczym, Mink, Maz, Olwock, Siedlce, and Garwolin. The battles east of Warsaw ended on September 15, 1939.

The Modlin Forts

The Panzerverband progressed as far as Maciejowice on the Vistula, passing through Stoczek, Zelechow, and Sobolew. On September 16, it received the order to move to the Modlin sector: after an exhausting march, the Panzerverband was rested over September 18 and 19. Subordinated to II. Armeekorps, it was then engaged against the Modlin Fortress. Since this was a siege proper, the main effort was naturally carried out by the artillery units, reinforced on the occasion by the Mörser-Batterie Beck that included a battery of 30.5-cm howitzers. The Germans had bypassed Warsaw and thrust southwest toward Naczpolsk whence the

A Deutschland defensive position on the Modlin front.

attacks began against Modlin's forts numbers 1 and 2, respectively to the west and northeast of the city. The fighting for the conquest of the Modlin forts lasted from September 19–29, 11 days of bloody, exhausting clashes that put the SS fighters to the test. The first few days saw reconnaissance patrols in action, sent ahead to probe the strength of the enemy defenses and above all to identify any weak points. The scouts paid a high price in blood to complete their missions. Then the actual attacks began, which saw the Deutschland pioneers opening gaps between the barbed wire and enemy bunkers. From above, Stuka dive-bombers supported the infantry attack.

On September 21, an assault troop including elements of the 3. Kompanie Deutschland carried out a scouting mission in the area west of Zacrozym. For courage demonstrated in the field, its

An SS motorcycle scout.

SS-Staf. Steiner with his general staff follows the course of the fighting against the Polish positions in Modlin.

A Deutschland defensive position on the Modlin front.

Fort 1 of the Modlin Fortress in Zacrozym, at the end of the fighting, September 1939.

commander, SS-Hstuf. Fritz Witt, was the first Panzerverband soldier to be decorated with the Iron Cross First Class. On the 22nd, the Modlin Fortress was definitively cut off from Warsaw, thanks to the critical intervention of the Stukas. The Panzerverband units eliminated the Polish defenses little by little.

During the night of September 27/28, an SS patrol reported that the garrison of Zacrozym Fort was showing signs of weakening and was on the verge of surrendering. A lightning surprise attack was therefore necessary. At dawn the next day, SS-Standartenführer Steiner personally led his men into an attack against the positions of Zacrozym and Modlin. By 0500, the forward elements had already penetrated the outer Polish defenses, ready to launch the final attack. The order came from headquarters to wait another hour, as the Poles were about to surrender. After an hour passed without any sign of surrender on the part of the enemy, the German artillery began to pummel Zacrozym and Fort Number 1. With assault teams armed with flamethrowers opening the way, the SS units broke through into Zacrozym occupying it completely after about an hour. The last of the Polish defenders took refuge in Fort Number 1. After a massive bombardment by the German artillery and by the Stukas, the garrison—including 1,200 officers and 24,000 soldiers and noncommissioned officers—was forced to surrender. At around 1200, Steiner was able to report to his headquarters that his battalions had achieved all their objectives. With the fall of the Modlin Fortress, the Deutschland Regiment's Polish campaign came to an end.

Deutschland soldiers near Fort 1 bunkers.

Deutschland soldiers near a Fort 1 bunker in Zacrozym, September 1939.

SS-Obf. Karl Maria Demelhuber.

Fritz Witt was born May 27, 1908, in Hohenlimburg, a suburb of the city of Hagen, SS-Nr. 21 518. He joined the SS in 1931, initially serving in the SS-Stabwache Berlin. On October 1, 1933, Witt was promoted to the rank of *SS-Untersturmführer*. In September 1934, he was promoted to *Obersturmführer* and shortly thereafter assumed command of the 3. Kompanie of the SS-Standarte Deutschland.

Johannes-Rudolf Mühlenkamp was born on November 8, 1910, in Metz-Montigny in Lorraine. On April 1, 1933, he joined the Allgemeine SS in the SS-Standarte 4 at Hartenholm, then in September 1934, he transferred to the SS-VT to SS-Standarte 2. He remained with this unit until in April 1935, he was sent to the first class of officer aspirants at the Führerschule in Braunschweig. He then attended a platoon leaders' course at Dachau between February–April 1936. Mühlenkamp was then posted as an officer to the new 15./Sta. Germania in early April of the same year and soon after underwent motorcycle training with the Heer's 2. Panzerdivision. His *Sturm* became the Kradschützen Kompanie Germania. From November 1, 1937 to May 1, 1938, Mühlenkamp trained as a platoon leader with II./Sta. Germania.

Hans Kempin was born June 7, 1913, in Berlin, SS-Nr. 51 240. Previously he had served in the 1./LSSAH and after attending the SS-Junkerschule in Bad Tölz, he moved to the 1./Sta. Deutschland.

Ferdinand Tietz was born December 19, 1903, in Bredinken in East Prussia, SS-Nr. 247 061. He had previously served as commander of 2./SS-Pi.Btl.2.

SS-Hstuf. Tietz, commander of the 2./SS-Pi.Btl.2 SS-VT on the Pilica River, near a destroyed bridge.

The Germania Regiment

On the night of August 16/17, 1939, the Germania Regiment was placed on alert and regrouped at the Königsbrück camp, where it came under the control of VIII. Armeekorps, which communicated the following orders to it: by September 2, 1939, at 0300, the Germania was to reach the sector between Althammer, Eichenkamp, Wieshuben, Kieferstädtel, and Graumannsdorf, and prepare to march in the direction of Nikolai. Entirely motorized, the SS regiment was to support 5. Panzerdivision.

On September 4, the regiment reached Myslowitz, despite destroyed bridges and mined roads, and continued its march in the direction of Sosnowice. On the 10th, the regiment was placed under the command of XXII. Armeekorps to be engaged at the bridgehead on the San River. Without the armored car platoon that had been attached to 5. Panzerdivision and minus the II./SS-Germania, which remained at the disposal of VIII. Armeekorps, SS-Staf. Demelhuber had to move with his troops on clogged roads and arrived with considerable delay in the XXII. Armeekorps operational sector, on the afternoon of September 12. He then received the order to protect the flanks of 2. Panzerdivision and 4. leichte-Division, between Jaworow and Sadowa Wisznia. In front of the Germania were the remains of the Polish units that had fought in Krakow and had entrenched themselves in the forests near the sector assigned to the regiment. At 0500 on September 13, the order came to take position.

Elements of the 15. Kompanie Germania waiting to cross a river. (Charles Trang Collection)

SS-Stubaf. Heinrich Köppen.

2. and 3. Kompanien were not present, having been left in reserve with XXII. Armeekorps in Wysocko. The 15.(Kradschtz.)Kp./SS-G of SS-Hstuf. Mühlenkamp blocked the Przemysl–Lviv road, in the direction of Sadowa Wisznia. At 1500, the SS units clashed with a Polish battalion fleeing eastward. The SS motorcyclists rushed the Poles and left them no time to react, capturing 500 soldiers with their officers. Meanwhile, the III./SS-G of SS-Stubaf. Köppen took up positions in the assigned sector. Toward evening, however, attacked by superior forces, the 15.(Kradschtz.)Kp./SS-G suffered heavy losses.

Contrary to what had happened in the afternoon, this time the Polish troops were well organized and were determined to break through the German lines to reach Warsaw. Mühlenkamp's men were forced to fall back north, to be supported by SS-Hstuf. Kempin's 1. Kompanie Germania, on both sides of Mala.

Polish antitank units in position, September 1939.

German troops crossing a bridge partially destroyed by the Poles.

German units cross the San River at Przemysl. Note at left, the mass of Polish prisoners.

German units on the streets of Warsaw.

On September 15, the regiment finally established contact with the motorized vanguard of XVII. Armeekorps. But immediately afterward, Polish forces of the 7th and 44th Infantry Divisions struck, overwhelming the III./SS-Germania and forcing it to fall back on Jaworow. Losses were high. Among the dead were SS-Stubaf. Köppen and SS-Hstuf. Schomberg.

A fresh defensive line was then established running from Mogila to the heights north of Tuczapy. Wave after wave, the attackers were repelled, but two assault groups managed to penetrate the SS positions. The regiment thus had to retreat to the area south of Jaworow, abandoning large quantities of equipment on the field. On the morning of September 17, the 7. Infanteriedivision finally arrived to ease the pressure on the SS units.

Meanwhile, II./SS-Germania, with Pz.Abw.Abt.8 in support, was still attached to 8. Infanteriedivision, and was ordered on September 12 to capture the bridge over the San River at Krzeszow. This meant a march of 80 kilometers on poor roads and, for the infantry divisions that followed, a two-day march. It took 11 hours to reach Kolbuszowa, before establishing contact with elements of 5. Panzerdivision. Without wasting any more time, II./SS-Germania continued its march in the direction of Rudnik, where it surprised a Polish cyclist unit. According to the prisoners' testimonies, the Krzeszow bridge was solidly defended, and explosive charges had already been set. SS-Ostubaf. Werner Dörffler-Schuband then decided to speed up the advance, sending a reconnaissance patrol toward the San River at Ulanowo.

Around midday, 5. Kompanie Germania captured the village of Konstantinowo, near Krzeszow and from there, continued in the direction of the bridge. The riverbank was secured,

German troops during the fighting in Warsaw.

but the SS units were unable to prevent the destruction of the bridge. Toward evening, at the head of a powerful assault group, SS-Ostuf. Jöckel managed to establish a bridgehead on the opposite bank. Before being blown up, the bridge had allowed numerous Polish soldiers to cross to the western bank of the San, but they were intercepted by 5. Kompanie at Nisko. II./SS-Germania was finally relieved on September 15. Refueled in the afternoon, it received orders to go to the aid of the main body of the regiment. The battalion arrived the next day in Przemysl and then Sadowa Wisznia. From here, it attacked the flanks of the massed Polish infantry who were attempting to retreat eastward. At the same time, they managed to free numerous SS POWs held in Mala.

On September 18, SS units were busy clearing the forests located in the area and at the same time, II./SS-Germania returned for attachment to the regiment. The battalion, exhausted by the fighting at Jaworow, was then sent to Krakow and from there arrived in Beraun, south of Prague, to be integrated into the SS-Verfügungstruppe-Division.

In Profile:
Otto Paetsch (1909–1945)

Otto Paetsch, SS Nr. 6143, was born in Rheinhausen on August 3, 1909. He studied theology at an evangelical school in Tübingen. In 1931 he joined the Allgemeine SS. In 1934 he was posted to SS-Standarte Germania, where he was promoted to *SS-Untersturmführer* on April 20, 1936, as a *Zugführer*. On April 20, 1940, Paetsch was promoted to *SS-Hauptsturmführer*. He took part in the invasion of Poland and the battle of France. At the end of 1940, he joined the newly established SS-Division Wiking and fought in Russia during Operation *Barbarossa*. From December 1941 he commanded the SS-Aufklärungs-Abteilung 5. On April 20, 1942, Paetsch was promoted to *SS-Sturmbannführer*. For bravery in the field, he was awarded the German Cross in Gold and was appointed commander of the SS-Panzer-Abteilung 10. In 1943 he was promoted to *SS-Obersturmbannführer* and was appointed commander of the SS-Panzerregiment 10. From June 1944 he fought on the Western Front. For his success at Avranches, and the breakout from the Falaise Pocket, he was awarded the Knight's Cross of the Iron Cross on August 23, 1944. In the autumn of 1944, he fought at Arnhem and in January 1945 in Lower Alsace. On March 16, 1945, he was killed in action near Altdamm. For the successful tank battles at Hagenau bridgehead, he was posthumously awarded the Oak Leaves to the Knight's Cross of the Iron Cross on May 4, 1945, and promoted to *SS-Standartenführer.*

A mortar platoon of 15. Kompanie Germania in Poland. In the center, with the cap, is SS Hstuf. Otto Paetsch.

Employment of the SS-Pionier-Bataillon

From August 24, 1939, the battalion was subordinated to General Hoth's XV. Armeekorps. This corps held the right flank of von Reichenau's Tenth Army: 2. leichte-Division was to attack in the van, having the Vistula as its initial objective. Afterward, the Polish forces were to be enveloped from the northeast. To do this, General Stumme's 2. leichte-Division received reinforcement from two companies of the SS-Pionier-Bataillon. At 0430 on September 1, 1939, the division crossed the border.

The SS pioneers were engaged immediately to neutralize minefields and eliminate roadblocks. But they failed to prevent the Poles from blowing up the bridge over the Malapane River. The 3. Kompanie engineers managed to get a temporary new bridge commissioned within an hour, an impressive feat. At the same time, construction of a 12-ton bridge began and was completed on the night of September 1/2. But by 0300, another bridge had been built by SS pioneers and allowed SS-Aufklärungs-Abteilung 7 to cross the river and reach the forest south of Kosiecin. Everywhere Polish forces began to fall back.

On September 3, the SS-Pionier-Bataillon set off again in the direction of Woischnik, at the disposal of the army corps. At 0700, an order came to repair a bridge, a mission that was completed in three hours. Soon afterward, General Hoth arrived in person to order the bridge located on the Koziklowy–Zarki road to be repaired. The battalion moved forward but found all the roads clogged with vehicles: the pioneers were then forced to carry a dismantled bridge on their own shoulders, moving on the sides of the road.

Once the mission was accomplished, the battalion arrived in Mijaczowo. On September 4, XV. Armeekorps intercepted the Polish rearguards and a large concentration of enemy troops in the Kielce sector. At 1045, the battalion received orders to clear the area around the Zarki–Lelow road. In this sector, the unit suffered its first casualty of the war, Herbert Norberger, a platoon commander in 3. Kompanie. The SS pioneers were also busy rebuilding the Woischnik and Smardzon bridges, completing the operation around 0200. Meanwhile, 2. leichte-Division captured the Szczekociny position, thus having the opportunity to attack the Kielce position.

On the night of September 4/5, the 3.Kp./SS-Pi.Btl. was placed under the control of Aufklärungs-Abteilung 29. Throughout September 5, SS pioneers were busy repairing the roads in the XV. Armeekorps area. The next day, the

SS-Hstuf. Karl Ullrich, commander of 3.Kp./SS-Pionier-Bataillon.

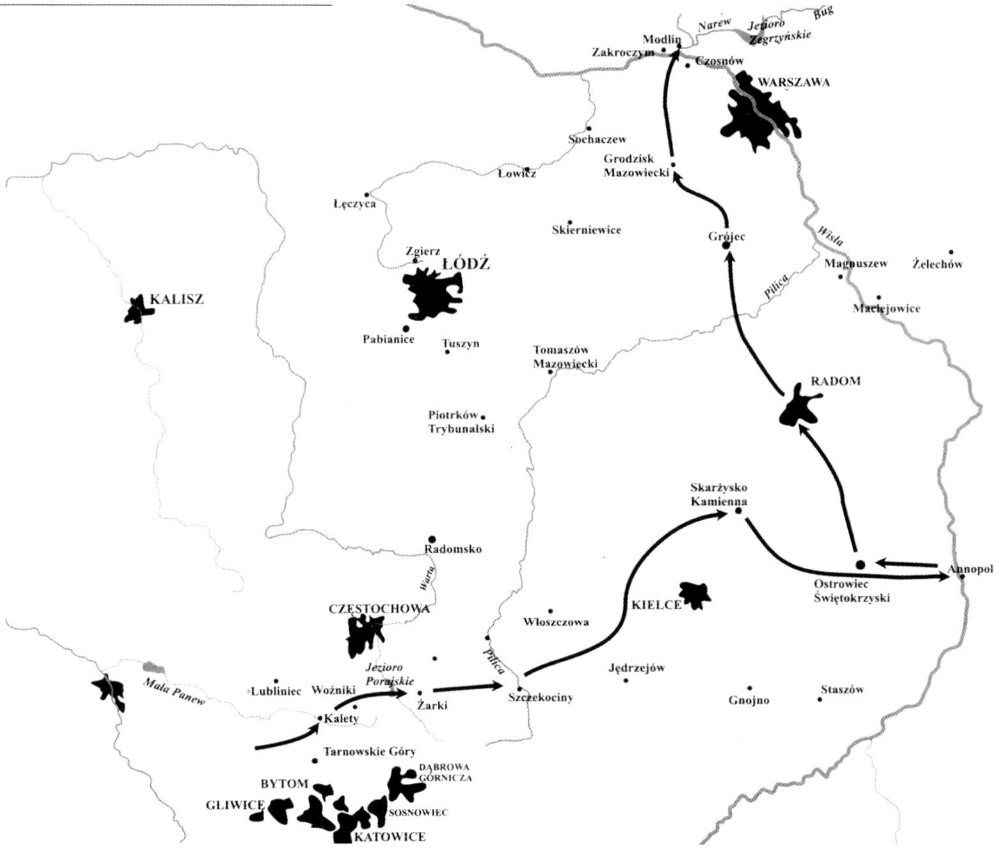

Movements of the SS-Pi.Btl. SS-VT in Poland, 1939.

corps regrouped on the Ostrowiec–Wierzlonik–Kamienna line to resume the advance in the direction of Radom. The SS-Pionier-Bataillon reached Kielce on September 8, and while XV. Armeekorps was moving toward Radom, the SS battalion took up positions between 2. and 3. leichte-Divisionen along the Ostrowiec–Brody line, to oppose any breakthrough attempts by the Poles. On September 9, units of XV. Armeekorps prevented the enemy from reaching the Vistula, before annihilating the Polish units surrounded in the Radom pocket. To this end, the SS-Pionier-Bataillon was engaged in securing the Debowa–Wola–Piaski line and the Kamienna–Brody sector. Two motorcycle companies from SS-Aufklärungs-Abteilung 7 arrived as reinforcements. On September 10, SS pioneers were busy clearing the forest north of Ostrowiec, between the Ostrowiec–Sicuno and Brody–Ilza roads. In the afternoon, the battalion was ordered to provide security for a major prisoner assembly center in Ostrowiec.

SS-Ostuf. Heinz Lammerding.

Pioneers of the 1.Kp./SS Pi.Btl. SS VT engaged in cutting logs to recover material for the construction of a bridge.

On September 11, the Poles began surrendering in entire companies. The SS battalion reported that they had captured the commander of the Polish 3rd Division. On September 13, with the annihilation of the Radom pocket done, the SS-Pionier-Bataillon received orders to build a bridge over the Vistula at Nowe. The whole unit got to work and by the afternoon of the next day, the bridge was completed.

On September 15, the SS-Pionier-Bataillon began repairs on the bridge over the Vistula at Annopol for IV. Armeekorps, an operation which was completed the following day. On September 19, the SS-Pionier-Bataillon arrived in Grodzisk. The next day, it was resubordinated to XV. Armeekorps, attached to the 29. Infanteriedivision to clear the forest north of Kaliszk. On the 21st, it cleared the Puszcza

Pioneers busy building a bridge.

Pioneers of the 2./SS Pi.Btl. SS VT, engaged in rebuilding a road bridge, September 1939.

Forest with its first two companies while the third was engaged in ensuring contact between 29. Infanteriedivision and 2. leichte-Division. On September 22, the bridge column was transferred to XIV. Armeekorps. The other companies continued to hunt down isolated Polish units. On September 23, while sweeps continued in the Puszcza–Kampinowska sector, the battalion was busy building a road to connect the 29. Infanteriedivision and 2. leichte-Division.

The Vistula bridge at Annopol, September 1939.

Infantry units and pioneers engaged in the attack against Warsaw, September 1939.

An assault group of the 1./SS-Pi.Btl. SS-VT.

On September 24, the SS-Pionier-Bataillon came under control of XIII. Armeekorps and 31. Infanteriedivision for the attack against Warsaw, from the southwest. The bulk of the battalion was subordinated to III. Infanterieregiment 17 engaged in the main assault, while 3. Kompanie was sent to reinforce II. Infanterieregiment 17 on the left.

On September 25, company commanders were informed of the manner of employment of their pioneers—to be organized into assault platoons in support of the infantry units. Their equipment—flamethrowers, smoke bombs, and explosive charges—had to always be available to neutralize obstacles, bunkers, and other points of resistance. The attack was launched on September 26 at 0745 and progressed well, but as the Germans approached the enemy positions they came under a massive artillery barrage. On the left flank, the 3. Kompanie pioneers suffered heavy losses, before reaching the enemy trenches and clearing them with hand grenades. The fighting lasted for seven hours. The Poles fought fiercely and Infanterieregiment 17 and the SS pioneers failed to achieve their objectives, with 3. Kompanie reporting four killed and nine wounded.

On the 27th, while the infantrymen and pioneers were preparing to attack again, news arrived that the Warsaw garrison had surrendered. On the 28th, the battalion was again attached to XV. Armeekorps in the Czechowice sector.

On October 1, it received orders to move to the Brdy Forest Camp, east of Pilsen, to be integrated into the SS-Verfügungstruppe-Division. On October 4, it arrived at Horowitz, where the new SS division was to be formed. There, the battalion was to form the nuclei for the creation of the pioneer battalions of the new SS divisions, in particular the SS-Totenkopf-Division and the Polizei-Division. Furthermore, numerous pioneers, thanks to the experience gained in the field, were sent to the Dresden school to serve as instructors at the SS-Pionier-Ersatz-Bataillon, whose command was entrusted to SS-Ostubaf. Blumberg. SS-Hstuf. Ferdinand Tietz took over the command of the SS-Pionier-Bataillon.

Aftermath

From effectively three regiments and several hodgepodge units on September 1, 1939, the Waffen-SS, or more properly at the time the SS-VT, was to grow into the juggernaut of 38 divisions of 900,000 troops that it would ultimately become. Regarded with much skepticism and derided by senior Heer officers as purely ceremonial troops incapable of blitzkrieg tactics, criticism was leveled at the Heer for the cynical misuse of the SS-VT units in the Polish campaign—although answerable to only Hitler, in military operations, Waffen-SS units were absorbed into the Heer order of battle. Poland was the Waffen-SS's rude baptism of fire against a Polish army that proved no pushover, despite being able to only mobilize well under half of an on-paper strength of a million men, and despite fielding antiquated armor and aircraft, a miniscule fleet, and cavalry that was utilized as mounted infantry.

Hitler visiting his loyal Leibstandarte units on the Polish front in September 1939: a warm handshake with Sepp Dietrich, in the presence of a smiling Max Wünsche.

Awarding decorations to the most deserving soldiers, 1939.

That the Waffen-SS displayed almost fanatical courage during the Polish campaign is beyond question, with the SS regiments earning several Iron Crosses Second Class, and the first Iron Cross First Class, by Panzerverband soldier SS-Hstuf. Fritz Witt, for his action at the Modlin Fortress. Many of the infamous Waffen-SS soldiers saw their first combat in Poland, with the likes of Paul Hausser, Sepp Dietrich, Fritz Witt, Hubert Meyer, Kurt "Panzer" Meyer, and dozens of others becoming almost household names in Germany after the campaign in the West in May 1940 and Operation *Barbarossa* a year or so later.

Considering that initially the SS-VT was reliant on the Heer for its recruits—often poor-quality army "rejects"—and its weaponry, again often second rate, it is astonishing what the SS soldiers were able to achieve in the face of Heer ambivalence and a gallant enemy. It was in Poland that the Waffen-SS had to learn "on the fly"—strategically but more importantly tactically, with many SS deaths attributed to clumsy leadership, as witnessed by some of Sepp Dietrich's rash tactical decisions. (Pro rata, SS deaths in combat exceeded considerably those of the Heer.)

The roll call of SS units in Poland makes for interesting study, with many of those first embryonic SS-VT units, such as the SS Heimwehr Danzig, fading away, while others grew into or merged with bigger SS units, such as the Leibstandarte SS Adolf Hitler, Panzerdivision Kempf (Panzerverband Ostpreußen), SS-Totenkopfdstandarte 4 Ostmark, SS-Standarte Germania, SS-Standarte Deutschland, and SS-Standarte Der Führer (although this latter was not engaged in Poland). And it wasn't only the SS infantry formations that distinguished themselves in Poland: the ancillary arms of artillery, reconnaissance, signals, and engineers gained invaluable experience on the battlefield, with the SS-Pionier-Bataillon excelling. It would be this mishmash of units and subunits that would go on to form the Waffen-SS of the Liebstandarte, the Totenkopf, the Das Reich, the Polizei, the Wiking, the Hohenstaufen, the Hitlerjugend, the Frundsberg, the Horst Wessel, and the Nordland, among many others. It was this almost million-strong "army within an army" that would become the scourge of Europe, on the Eastern Front and on the Western Front, for almost six long years.

Delivery to the Führer of a banner captured from a Polish unit, September 1939.

Further Reading

Books

Afiero, Massimiliano. *2.SS-Panzerdivision "Das Reich" Vol. I: 1939–1943*. Associazione Culturale Ritterkreuz.

Afiero, Massimiliano. *3.SS-Panzerdivision "Totenkopf" Vol. I: 1939–1943*. Associazione Culturale Ritterkreuz.

Afiero, Massimiliano. *Leibstandarte Adolf Hitler Vol. I: 1933–1943*. Associazione Culturale Ritterkreuz.

Afiero, Massimiliano. *Waffen SS in guerra Vol. I: 1939–1943*. Associazione Culturale Ritterkreuz.

Agte, Patrick. *Jochen Peiper: Commander Panzerregiment Leibstandarte*. Winnipeg: Fedorowicz, 1999.

Baxter, Ian. *SS Das Reich At War 1939–1945*. Barnsley: Pen & Sword, 2017.

Bishop, Chris, ed. *The Encyclopedia of Weapons of World War II*. New York: Metro Books, 2002.

Butler, Rupert. *SS-Leibstandarte: The History of the First SS division 1933–45*. London: Amber Books, 2001.

Duprat, François. *Les campagnes de la Waffen SS*. Paris: Les Sept Couleurs, 1973.

Fritz, Stephen G. *Frontsoldaten: The German Soldier in World War II*. Lexington: University Press of Kentucky, 1995.

Gefährten unserer Jugend: Die Flak-Abteilung der Leibstandarte. Preussisch Oldendorf: Verlag Schütz, 1984.

Hausser, Paul. *Waffen SS im Einsatz*. Göttingen: Plesse Verlag, 1953.

Landemer, Henri. *La Waffen SS*. Paris: Balland, 1972.

Lehmann, Rudolf. *Die Leibstandarte: Volumes 1–3*. Osnabrück: Munin Verlag, 1977–1982.

Liddell Hart, B. H. *Storia militare della seconda guerra mondiale*. Milan: Mondadori, 1996.

Lucas, James and Matthew Cooper. *Hitler's Elite: Leibstandarte SS*. London: Macdonald & Jane's, 1975.

Lumsden, Robin. *La vera storia delle SS*. Rome: Newton & Compton Editori, 2017.

Meyer, Kurt. *Grenadiers*. Mechanicsburg: Stackpole Books, 2005.

Michaelis, Rolf. *Die Waffen SS: mythos und wirklichkeit*. Berlin: Michaelis-Verlag, 2006.

Nafziger, George F. *The German Order of Battle: Infantry in World War II*. London: Greenhill Books, 2000.

Solarz, Jacek. *SS-Verfügungstruppen 1939*. Poland: Wydawnictwo Militaria, 2001.

Special Series. *No. 8 German Tactical Doctrine*. Military Intelligence Service, 1942.

Stein, George H. *The Waffen-SS: Hitler's Elite Guard at War 1939–1945*. Ithaca: Cornell University Press, 1944.

Steiner, Felix. *Die Freiwilligen: Idee und Opfergang*. Plesse Verlag, Göttingen, 1958.

Tessin, Georg. *Verbande und truppen der deutschen Wehrmacht und Waffen-SS*. Germany: Biblio Verlag, 1965.

Trang, Charles. *Dictionnaire de la Waffen SS*, Volumes 1–4. Saint-Martin-des-Entrées: Editions Heimdal, 2011–14.

Trang, Charles. *Leibstandarte 1933–1942*. Saint-Martin-des-Entrées: Editions Heimdal, 2008.
Tucker-Jones, Anthony. *Hitler's Armed SS: The Waffen-SS at War, 1939–1945*. Barnsley: Pen & Sword Military, 2022.
Weidinger, Otto. *Division Das Reich. Der Weg der 2. SS-Panzerdivision "Das Reich": Die Geschichte der Stammdivision der Waffen-SS. Band I*. Germany: Munin-Verlag, 1967.
Weingartner, James. *Hitler's Guard: The Story of the Leibstandarte SS Adolf Hitler, 1933–1945*. Carbondale: Southern Illinois University Press, 1990.
Williamson, Gordon. *Storia Illustrata delle SS*. Rome: Newton & Compton Editori, 2007.
Zaloga, Steven J. *L'invasione della Polonia*. Oxford: Osprey Publishing, 2009.

Magazines

Der grosse deutsche feldzug gegen Polen. Vienna, 1939.
Hoffmann, Heinrich. *Mit Hitler in Polen*. Berlin, 1939.
Landgraf, Hugo. *Kampf um Danzig*. Dresden, 1940.
Das Schwarze Korps magazine, various numbers.
Fronti di Guerra bimonthly magazine dedicated to the formations of the Axis Forces in World War II, various numbers.
Ritterkreuz bimonthly magazine dedicated to the Waffen-SS, various numbers.
Signal magazine, various editions and numbers.

Public Archives

Bundesarchiv Berlin Lichterfelde, Germany.
Bundesarchiv-Militärarchiv Freiburg, Germany.
U.S. National Archives Washington, United States.
Vojensky Historicky Archiv Praga, Czech Republic.

Index